The Team Guide to

Continuous

Improvement

The Foundation of Lean Organization

A System of Total Engagement in Performance Improvement

By
Lawrence M. Miller

Published by
Miller Management Press, LLC
ISBN Number: 978-0-578-11546-7

TABLE OF CONTENTS

HOW TO USE THIS WORKBOOK:

For the past thirty years I have written and re-written, and re-written... you get the idea... a workbook for employee and management teams. This may be my tenth version, but who's counting. Every couple of years I revise it based on my experience working with clients and any feedback I receive. If you have my *Lean Team Management* or *HealthCare Lean* books you will find that most of the material is the same, just revised... continuously improved.

This workbook is intended to be used in a flexible, just-in-time, on-the-spot manner. The chapters are organized in what have proven to be reasonably sized training modules. They are also organized into the major issues facing teams. Training materials, forms and PowerPoint's are available from the author for each chapter.

There is no one right sequence for presenting these modules and developing teams. For example, some teams may already have been trained in facilitation skills or team dynamics. Their priority may be getting down to solving problems and improving performance. In other cases, it would be wise to take the time to develop decision styles, facilitation and team dynamics before starting the serious work of improving performance.

This workbook has been used most successfully when there is a trainer/coach assigned to each team. This coach not only presents the training modules, but also assists in the completion of deliverables, provides direct coaching and feedback to the team and its leaders. This feedback is almost always essential in the successful development of the team process.

The author has customized this manual for clients who wish to make it their own when training a significant number of employees.

Please contact me (LMMiller@lmmiller.com) if you have any questions or suggestions. Also, you may benefit from my blog posts in which I share experience in the application of these methods (www.ManagementMeditations.com).

INTRODUCTION

You will either continuously improve or go out of business. Those who are best at continuous improvement are those who will thrive in global competition. Those who are best at continuous improvement will engage everyone, and I mean everyone, in an on-going process of thinking, analyzing, experimenting, and standardizing improvements. Whether at the level of senior management, engineering, marketing, research and development, or production teams, the practices and skills are similar. This workbook is about developing those practices as habit in your organization.

The team in an organization is like the family in a society. It is the fundamental building block of trust and competence. Lean organizations are a social system, a culture, as well as a technical system. At the heart of that social system is the small work group, the team, both at the front line level and at all levels of management. It doesn't matter whether your organization is entirely comprised of knowledge workers, service providers in a not-for-profit organization, or assembly line workers in a manufacturing plant; the most effective organizations are all built on the foundation of effective teams.

The term "lean" is used throughout this book. It originated in a study of the world's best manufacturing organizations, particularly the auto assembly plants of Toyota and Honda. A group at MIT studied the differences between those auto plants producing the highest quality cars and achieving the greatest efficiency, versus those who were not. They called these "lean plants" because the term "lean" implied the elimination of unnecessary activities. And, here is what they found at the heart of those plants.

"What are the truly important organizational features of a lean plant - the specific aspects of plant operations that account for up to half of the overall performance differences among plants across the world? The truly lean plant has two key organizational features: It transfers the maximum number of tasks and responsibilities to those workers actually adding value to the car on the line, and it has in place a system for detecting defects that quickly traces every problem, once discovered, to its ultimate cause....So in the end, *it is the dynamic work team that emerges as the heart of the lean factory.*"[1]

---

[1] Womack, J.P., Jones, D. T., and Roos D. *The Machine That Changed the World.* New York: Rawson Associates, 1990, P. 99.

It is important to know that after more than forty years of practice at lean manufacturing, Toyota managers and front-line employees are everyday seeking to find ways to improve how they do their work. They are actively engaged in continuous improvement. They are still on the journey to find the ideal way to build cars. Your journey will not be completed in six months or a year. It will become a way of life and last for your entire career. You may as well become good at it.

This manual is an attempt to present the most essential practices of effective work groups and managing teams. It is intended for teams at every level of the organization. It is based on both best practices in lean organizations and the history of self-directed or high performance teams. This manual provides the structure, skills and practices that have proved to be the foundation of lean organization. That foundation is an organization in which employees at every level serve on teams that manage their own work; serve the customers who receive their work; give feedback to their suppliers; and continuously seek to improve their process. The goal is to empower every team by making them the "world's greatest experts" in their own work.

It is important to understand what continuous improvement is and is not. Continuous improvement for most companies is a change in culture.

- Continuous improvement is a culture of responsibility for performance at every level of the organization.
- It is a culture of respect for employees, a belief that the "world's greatest experts are on-the-spot."
- It is a culture that is very focused on data, the facts of performance.
- It is a culture of experimentation and learning.
- It requires everyone to know and serve their customers, internally and externally.
- It is a culture of competence in decision-making and group problem-solving.
- It is continually seeking to eliminate non-value adding activity, waste, and replace it with effort that adds value.

And, perhaps most importantly, it is a culture that must be practiced by managers as well as employees.

Each of these characteristics is true of any genuinely lean organization. Lean is not a set of problem-solving techniques. Lean is a culture that is practiced top-to-bottom, left-to-right, in the organization.

CHAPTER 1

CHANGE MANAGEMENT: WHOLE-SYSTEM ARCHITECTURE

Sometimes change is not continuous. Rather, it may be revolutionary, a complete rethinking of how we do our work. Sometimes it is not incremental change, one small experiment at a time, but a change in the whole system of the organization.

I was speaking at a Toyota supplier's conference a few years back and observed a presentation by the president of one of Toyota's U.S. suppliers. He was a young man and a bit nervous in his presentation. He had been offered help by Toyota and was visibly shaken from the experience. Toyota has an internal consulting group that works with their suppliers. This group is made up of highly experienced lean experts, experts in the Toyota Production System.

This young president described how the Toyota change agents had required that he give them free reign in his plant and that he would stand to the side while they redesigned the work flow and job assignments. They shut the plant down for about one week. He stood by in horror as the Toyota engineers literally ripped his equipment out of the floor, re-arranged every piece of gear, changed the flow of the work and redefined the jobs of everyone in the plant, including himself! It was not what he regarded as a warm and fuzzy experience. It produced a revolution in how they did their work.

At lunch I sat with these Toyota consultants and discussed how they go about their work. For many years I had been implementing change in the processes and culture of organizations, but this conversation made me question my own methods. I explained to them that when I go into a client organization I ask the senior managers to form a steering committee and write a charter for change that defines the goals, principles, boundaries, etc. I then form design teams of frontline employees and managers and I then facilitate the process by which they redesign both their technical system (work flow) and their social system that includes how decisions are made, the organization structure, teams, sources of motivation, etc.

They looked puzzled. They asked me why I would ask them to redesign their own work. I explained that in our culture it was important to gain "buy-in" and commitment. Then, one of these Japanese engineers looked at me and said rather forcefully and unapologetically, "But, they don't know! We do know! Asking them would be useless."

It took me a while to put this in perspective. Clearly, these Toyota manufacturing engineers did know. They knew how to layout the equipment and assign work in a plant that bends metal, repetitively, every day. But, at the same time the owner of the company was traumatized by the event.

This was not continuous improvement. This was radical, revolutionary, and whole-system change, imposed from outside the organization. In our culture, in which most of the employees are well educated and highly motivated, you must engage them in the co-creation of change, even when it is revolutionary change.

Many organizations today are in need of revolutionary change, but it must be a revolution that is created from within.

WHOLE-SYSTEM ARCHITECTURE

There are two types of change that can lead to lean processes and lean culture. One is "Whole-System Architecture" in which you step back and consider the entire system of the organization and ask fundamental questions. Why do we do this process at all? What is our core work? How does this add value? You consider the current state and design the future state of both the technical system, the work flow, and the social system that surrounds and enables that work flow. Too many lean implementations are focused solely on the technical system and fail to redesign the social system. The problems in organizations are more likely to be the result of a social system that fails to encourage innovation, teamwork and open dialogue then any particular failure of a work process.

Whole-System Architecture presents a useful metaphor. When you walk into a great cathedral your head goes back and you look up into the heavens of stained glass and flying buttresses. You marvel at the construction. And your first impulse is to focus on the physical thing of the structure. But, the architect had an end in mind. The architect understood that the nature of physical space, the interior structure of the cathedral, has an effect on the human spirit, emotions, and possibly behavior. And, so too does the structure of your organization. But in most cases the effect is unintentional and often stifling, rather than uplifting of the human spirit. We must become architects of our organizations to promote the spirit of service to customers and the habits of innovation.

Changing the culture means changing "real stuff" that drives behavior. One way of addressing these is to address the 5S's of any organization – **Structure, Systems, Skills, Style** and **Symbols**. These five S's should not be confused with the 5S's that are most often promoted to create an orderly workplace. While those are important, they do not address the most important things that drive the culture.

Macro and Micro Lean Implementation

Whole-System Architecture	Continuous Improvement
✓ Revolutionary/Re-Engineering ✓ Rethinking the Whole-System ✓ Big System Change to create major improvements ✓ Questioning why we do everything ✓ Changes in both work systems and social systems ✓ Must begin and end with the customer view ✓ Involves all stakeholders including the customer ✓ Design with the changing landscape in mind ✓ Rethinking Organization Structure	✓ Evolutionary ✓ Change within a stable system ✓ Gradual & small improvements ✓ Generally changes in the work process ✓ Questioning how we can best do everything. ✓ May be internal process focused or customer focused ✓ Done by those doing the work at every level ✓ Process owners experiment and improve ✓ How to improve work within the current structure

You cannot fix the work processes unless you fix the culture. All current deficiencies in your work process are derived from cultural assumptions and behavior. The root cause is the culture, and particularly the culture of management.

The basic structure of organizations often creates silos that prevent teamwork. The purpose of organization structure is to enhance the flow of work, not to inhibit that flow. How are medical teams organized? Are they organized by specialty, by geography, by patient population? Is there only one team structure or are their multiple structures that promote different types of knowledge sharing and decision-making? Structure matters. Most continuous improvement efforts attempt to work within existing structures and fail to ask fundamental questions about the nature of our organizations.

The systems of information flow are similar to the nervous system in the body, constantly sending messages that trigger behavior and emotions. The systems of hiring, reward and recognition, promotion, training and development, budgeting and sharing financial information all drive performance. Who designed these systems? When they did, what was their intention or philosophy? Were they designed to maximize decision-making ability of front line team members? Were they designed to promote teamwork? Do they reinforce experimentation and continuous improvement? It is likely that they do not. And, it is even more likely that they were each designed by experts in IT, HR or Finance who were focused on their expert knowledge, and not focused on achieving the outcome of superior patient care. They were not integrated as a whole-system with common purpose and principles. They are most likely "dis-integrated" and misaligned and that is the cause of a huge amount of waste in our organizations.

The purpose of whole system change is to align the systems, structure and other factors to promote teamwork and continuous improvement, to knock down the walls that interrupt flow and create delays and waste. All systems should be aligned to serve the needs of patients or customers.

You can think of Whole-System Architecture as "Macro Lean." And it should generally come before the process of continuous improvement. But, we aren't always that smart and we discover the need for changes in systems and structure along the path of continuous improvement. For this reason I recommend that there be an internal culture strategy team that studies the architecture of the organization and makes design recommendations.

Implementing Lean & Continuous Improvement

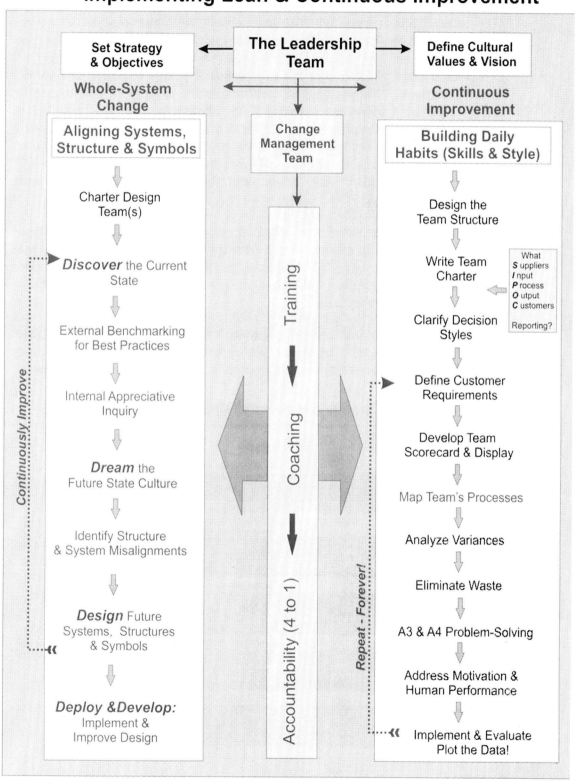

A critical component of Whole-System Architecture is the psychology of co-creation. In numerous organizations I have had design teams go visit with their customers or ask their customers to come meet with the design team. The customers are simply asked, "How can we better meet your needs? What changes would you like to see in how we serve you?" No customer has ever objected to this question. The second question is, "Will you give us feedback on the process we redesign to be sure that it meets your needs?" They always answer "Yes." The act of engaging the customer in the design of the process that will serve them is the best "sales call" your organization will ever make. It never fails. When they feel that you are listening to them and changing to meet their needs, they will support your efforts and feel a greater bond with your organization.

The exact same psychology of co-creation is true with employees and managers in all functions. When the managers of any group in any organization seek to listen and design their work to meet the needs of their customers, they will immediately gain greater support from those customers. It never fails.

I worked with a major Southern university to redesign all of their business services that served both their hospital complex and their academic departments and student body. At the outset, these two major

University Campus and Hospital Center Business Services

groups of customers both were extremely dissatisfied with the services they received from human resources, information technology, property management, and financial services. I encouraged them to listen deeply to their customer's expression of their needs, rather than their own assumptions and belief in their own expertise. They went out and interviewed the Chairs of each academic department and the leaders of each department or function in the hospital complex. They then not only redesigned each of their core processes to better meet their customer's needs, they also restructured their own management team so that the leaders of each major process served as a member of the management team. They became process owners and process focused.

It is hard to say which had a greater effect on the satisfaction of the hospital and academic staff – the actual improvements in the work process, or the simple fact of being fully engaged in co-creating those services.

FROM WHOLE-SYSTEM TO CONTINUOUS IMPROVEMENT

When the revolution is over the hard work begins. Most revolutions in nations fail to produce the future desired by the revolutionaries. Why? Because the habits of daily life were conditioned by the old system. My son was in Iraq working on building the first election process after the fall of Saddam Hussein. One night on Skype I asked him the question everyone wanted to know. "Do you think this will really work?" His answer was equally simple: "Yes, if they can just learn to listen to each other." He explained that during the days of Saddam anyone in a position of responsibility had learned not to say what they really thought, but to say what they thought was safe. If those habits continued and if they could not truly listen and talk to each other, democracy cannot work.

Democracy requires a whole-system. It requires the laws and structure of an election process. But, it also requires a way of life – a way of thinking and acting in which the citizens take responsibility for their own government. It is not so easy.

Lean management, whether in manufacturing or health care, first requires a system in which decisions can be made by those who do the work. It requires the systems of information sharing and the structures of teams that knock down walls within the core work process. But, then it requires the effort and the habits of every member of every team, from top to bottom, to practice shared decision-making, a focus on data, a focus on the needs of customers, and the continual experimentation that is at the heart of lean management.

The purpose of the remainder of this book is to assist you in the development of those habits.[2]

CASE STUDY AND EXERCISE:

Read the following case study and ask yourself, which elements of the Honda Way would represent a revolutionary change or an evolutionary change for my organization?

Which elements of the Honda Way require changes in systems and structure and which require changes in skills and style, human behavior?

THE HONDA WAY: A VISIT TO MARYSVILLE

I wrote the following case study, I believe, in 1989. Many of the details may be out of date. However, the important lessons of building and aligning a culture will never be out of date.

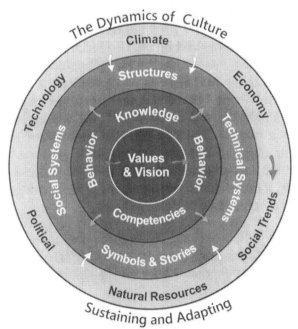

As you read this you may wish to consider your own culture and how it has been designed to maximize human performance, quality and customer satisfaction. The following graphic is one way to describe the influences, internal and external, on the culture of any organization. I organized my observations as I visited Honda's plant according to this model.

During the early days of Honda America Manufacturing's operations in Marysville, Ohio, they used my book *American Spirit* as a management development text. This resulted in several invitations to visit and present to the Honda management group and supplier groups. I wrote the following after my first two day visit to the Marysville plants.

I spent two days touring the plants, speaking with managers and production associates, sitting in on meetings, and asking lots of questions. Why is Honda so good? The answer is both simple and complex. It is a

---

[2] More information on Whole-System Architecture can be found in *Lean Culture – The Leader's Guide.*

combination of technical, or work process design; and, their unique culture.

There is nothing that stands out as their single secret to quality. The secret is - they do everything -and they do it as a team!

I find that in every healthy corporate culture there is a common understanding of philosophy, the values and visions upon which decisions and practices are based. The management practices, the structure, systems, skills, style, and symbols are consistent with the philosophy. At Honda there is clearly a "Team" culture.

Even before entering the building, the philosophy became evident. As we drove toward the plant I noticed lines of newly planted trees. I was told that they were planted by newly hired associates. Each new associate plants a tree "so they can grow with the company." All associates (the term used for all employees) know the company philosophy. They see it every day in a hundred ways. They hear it consistently from their leaders. There are no contradictions.

The president of Honda of America is Shoichiro Irimajiri, known as Mr. Iri by the associates. Earlier in his career, Mr. Iri was responsible for managing Honda's successful racing efforts, designing engines and managing production facilities in Japan. He frequently speaks of the "Racing Spirit." The Racing Spirit includes five principles:

1. *Seek the challenger.*
2. *Be ready on time.*
3. *Teamwork.*
4. *Quick Response.*
5. *Winner Takes All!*

Perhaps more instructive of the Honda philosophy is his story of one of his early racing efforts.

It was in 1965 when Mr. Iri was working on the Formula One racing engines. In the British Grand Prix of that year, the engine failed and it was torn down and examined by Mr. Honda himself.

Examining the failed piston he turned to Shoichiro Irimajiri and demanded, "Who designed this piston?" "I did," he acknowledged. After examining the engineering drawing Mr. Honda roared out, 'You! Stupid! No wonder the piston gets burned. You have changed the thickness here."

After the young Irimajiri attempted to defend his design change with some data from previous engines, Mr. Honda roared again: "I hate college graduates! They use only their heads. Do you really think you can use such obsolete data obtained from old, low-performance engines? I have been making and designing pistons for several years. I am fully aware how critical half a millimeter is here. A company does not need people like you who use only their heads. Before you laid out this design, why didn't you listen to opinions of those experienced people in the shop? If you think academic study in college is everything, you are totally wrong. You will be useless in Honda unless you spend more time on-the-spot for many years to come."

"You will go to the machining shop," Mr. Honda ordered the young engineer, "and you will apologize to every person there, for you have wasted their efforts." Mr. Honda followed him down the hall to make sure he did as directed. Mr. Iri recalls that he was only glad that he had no ambition of becoming president of the company. He was not even sure he would succeed as an engineer. He learned his lesson. He not only succeeded as an engineer, designing several successful racing engines, but he became the president of Honda of America, the first Japanese company to export cars back to Japan. Shoichiro Irimajiri still listens to those experienced people in the shop and he is not wasting their time.

The Honda philosophy stresses to be on-the-spot in the plant and see the problem, touch the part, and gain experience in the actual job, in order to effectively solve a problem.[3] Engineers and management spend most of their time in the factory, in touch with their associates, the product, and the process. The Honda philosophy is manifested in all of the management practices. In the symbols, structure, systems, skills, and style[4], the philosophy can be seen and experienced every day, by every employee, every hour.

SYMBOLS:

When I arrived at the Marysville plant I was given a uniform to wear in the plant. I was told that this wasn't given to all guests, only "honored guests." To cover my tie with the white smock with the Honda name, to look the same as every other associate, was an honor. I can assure you that by the time my visit was finished it felt like an honor. To be part of a proud group of people, to share their symbol of equality, caused me to feel a part, invested, in their shared goals.

All associates, from president to newest hired associate, eat in the same cafeteria, park in the same undesignated parking spaces, and

---

[3] In recent years this has become known as the "Gemba" walk.

[4] These five "S's" have been used by me and others as a structure for organization design, or "socio-technical systems" design.

managers sit at the same metal desks in open office areas. Most of the desks are arranged in blocks of six, often with paired Japanese and American managers sitting across from one another. All of the managers of the motorcycle plant sit at one block of six identical desks, the Japanese vice-president and the American plant manager sitting across from each other.

As I walked through the plant, the cleanest non-food manufacturing plant out of several hundred I have been in, I observed a vice-president stop and pick up a misplaced object on the floor. There is nothing on the floor. There are also no maintenance people to clean up! Everyone, every associate and manager, cleans his or her own work area.

To many, these symbols will seem trivial. They would be if they stood alone, at odds with the behavior and attitudes of the people, or if the structure and systems stood in contradiction. However, they are one part of a total system, like a well-engineered engine with all components balanced and moving in unison. Symbols, structure, systems, skills and style are all aligned.

STRUCTURE:

Everyone is a member of a team. The team is the first level of organization. At 6:30 AM each day, every associate meets with his team and team leader. The day's work is discussed and feedback on the previous day's quality is given. Any problems, changes, or concerns are shared during this meeting.

A team is comprised of 15 to 20 associates who work in a common area. As I toured both the auto and motorcycle plant, I stood and watched the assembly line in operation. I asked which person was the team leader and which was the production coordinator, the second-level manager. It was very hard to find them or distinguish them. I watched as there was an apparent problem on the motorcycle line.

One employee, having difficulty getting a frame over an engine assembly, had stopped the line. He and another associate worked frantically to get the frame in place. It took about twenty seconds for the line to move again. I asked where the team leader was. The other associate, helping to form the frame, was the team leader. The production coordinator was at the next station on the assembly line helping another associate catch up on the placement of electrical wire assemblies. I watched for about fifteen minutes as the team leader and production coordinator (equivalent of first-line supervisor and department manager) worked on the line, smiling, joking, and working hard and fast with their associates.

Nowhere is there a private office for team leaders or production coordinators. They do not remove themselves from the work. They are on-the-spot, seeing and touching the product, gaining experience and solving problems. They are part of the working team.

All managers are organized into teams and solve problems together. The structure of the organization, as well as the physical arrangement of desks and offices, makes group problem-solving a natural and constant occurrence.

Participation in the continuous improvement process is also structured through Quality Circles. NH Circles (NH stands for "Now Honda, New Honda, Next Honda") are similar to quality circles in many other companies. However, at Honda they are one component of a total involvement process which they call of VIP (Voluntary Involvement Program).

VIP includes a suggestion system, quality awards, and safety awards. Twenty percent of all associates participate in circles. The rate of suggestion adoption is 59.4 percent, and 60 percent participate in some component of the VIP process. In speaking with several NH Circle members, I was impressed that they felt the responsibility to see that accepted recommendations for improvement were implemented. They also felt that their circles were different from those in other companies in that they are constantly looking for any improvement in the production process, large or small, and even small improvements are highly valued. They said that the success of Honda was the result of constantly finding small improvements, not just looking for major ones.

System:

I expected to find systems of employee involvement at Marysville. However, I was somewhat surprised to see the amount of thought put into the positive reinforcement systems. Honda of America practices performance management, or as I used to call it "behavior management." They have found ways to provide constant feedback, recognition, and tangible positive reinforcement for almost every form of desirable performance.

The NH Circle program, suggestion system, quality awards, and safety awards are all tied together with a point system. Every associate earns points by participating in any of these improvement processes. Awards include award certificates, gift certificates, Department Manager's Award, Plant Manager's Award, and President's Award. These also result in points accumulating over your career, and these points can earn a Honda Civic (that's for 2,500 points) and an Accord (5,000 points), plus two weeks off with pay and airplane tickets to anywhere in the world with spending money.

In addition to hourly or salaried compensation, all associates participate in profit sharing. This profit sharing is an innovation of Honda of America and is not part of the system in Japan. Ten percent of the gross profit generated by Honda Motor Company is shared with associates based on their relative compensation. Good attendance results in another bonus. The average bonus check for attendance in 1986 was $832. The average profit sharing check was $2,688.

Performance analysis and feedback is an important part of any total performance management system. In each of the open office areas and in each of the many conference rooms, all of the walls are literally covered with charts and graphs representing different quality and productivity performance variables. The graphs are of every possible variety, some employing Statistical Process Control methods and some simply reflecting historical data with means, trends, and goal lines. Frequently, along with the charts on the wall are lists of causes or solutions to problems. Diagrams of auto parts or production machinery with arrows pointing to sources of problems are also frequent. It is obvious that all of the managers at Honda are in touch with plant performance data.

Another system worthy of mention is the discipline system. There are some fairly traditional and sound procedures for gradual counseling and discipline. However, the unique part of the discipline process is the peer review provided for associates who are dismissed for poor conduct. If an associate wishes to appeal a termination, a peer review panel is formed by randomly selecting six or eight production associates. One senior manager also serves on the panel with equal vote. The panel hears both sides of the case and then decides to overturn or accept the management decision. Nine out of ten times the decisions are upheld by the associates.

SKILLS:

The measure of skills is found in the work product. There is no question Honda has highly skilled engineering and quality personnel. Most engineers are Japanese. Hiring and training more Americans is a goal for coming years. Honda is an engineering company. Most of the Japanese senior managers have served as design engineers for engines, including racing engines, or other components.

Having worked at other auto companies, it soon became obvious to me that at Honda the most valued personnel are those with engineering and technical competence. At many other companies, it is the financial managers and management professionals who are most valued. Honda is in the business of making excellent cars. Many other companies are in the business of making money, and, only secondarily, making cars. Honda makes money and does not need layers of bureaucratic managers because they are passionately dedicated to their technology and products.

On the assembly line, there is a process of continual skill development. Associates are rotated from one position to another to broaden their skills and increase their flexibility. Even when applicants are interviewed for employment at Honda, they are asked questions to determine their flexibility. Flexibility and the development of broad-based skills is a central principle.

At Honda, it is assumed the production associates are intelligent, skilled, and dedicated. They can, therefore, be trusted to manage the quality process. Every associate is a quality control inspector. The assembly process at Honda is based on just-in-time (JIT) inventory and assumption of 100 percent quality parts. Each associate knows it is his or her job to inspect each part to assure conformance to requirements. Any associate can reject a part. If a manager wants the part used after the associate has rejected it, the burden is on the manager to explain to the associate why it should be used. There is a quality assurance department with a team of associates who will call the suppliers regarding any and every bad part. Every vendor is assigned to one associate, who knows exactly who to call, including home telephones, to provide immediate feedback on any deviation from quality requirements.

STYLE:

All of the methods described above are held together by people with a sense of humor and a high level of people-to-people skills.

As I interviewed managers, I repeatedly asked them how they felt working for, or with, Japanese managers. I wanted to know if there was any resentment toward the Japanese. I could find absolutely none. I could only find the most sincere respect and friendship. There was no feeling of "us Americans" working for "them." The reason for this mutual respect became clear the next morning.

Every morning the 10 or 12 managers of the motorcycle plant meet to review performance, solve problems, and make plans for the day. The Japanese vice-president responsible for the motorcycle operations sat at the end of the table. The meeting was led by a manager who was two levels down. There was a lively discussion about the handling of an "almost-in-time" inventory situation that had almost halted production the previous day. There were three or four Japanese managers and about eight Americans in the meeting. One of the Japanese managers was very vocal about how confusing the situation was and how it should have been handled better. Several others discussed what happened and how it was being resolved today. The vice-president sat quietly through a half hour of discussion, never saying anything until the meeting was coming to a conclusion. Only then did he speak out. He had two points. First, he wanted to thank everyone for their efforts yesterday, rising to meet the challenge presented by their problem. Second, he wanted to stress how important it was to meet another challenge that was coming up within the next week. His tone was calm and reassuring.

These incidents, and dozens of others like them, proved to me that the integration of cultures is working in Marysville. The Americans have adopted the Japanese patience and view things from a long-term perspective. The Japanese have adopted, or at least accepted, the American fun-loving familiarity and creativity.

The style at Honda is different than at other Japanese companies and this may be central to their success and initiative in manufacturing in the United States. The traditional Japanese company places a high value on age and seniority. Honda does not. Mr. Irimajiri is a young man excited by winning races and building racing engines. Mr. Honda has retired because he believes the company should be run by young men. The first principle of Honda management policy is: "Proceed always with ambition and youthfulness." The second is: "Respect sound theory, develop fresh ideas and make the most effective use of time." The third is: "Enjoy your work, and always brighten your working atmosphere."

Honda now employs 6,000 youthful-minded and creative Buckeye associates in Marysville. That number will be raised to over 8,000 as the second auto assembly plant is built nearby.[5] The U.S.-manufactured content of the Honda Accord is now about 60 percent and will be increased to 75 percent. The Accord is more American than some GM, Ford, or Chrysler nameplates with higher imported content.

As I left Marysville, I didn't leave with the feeling that I had visited a "foreign" manufacturer. Rather, I had the feeling that I had visited something new. I had visited a world-embracing company, with a world-embracing philosophy, as much American as Japanese, perhaps the best of both world. I could also think of nothing that Honda was doing, no secret in either principle or practice, which could not be adopted by any company - if its senior managers were knowledgeable, committed, and would "proceed always with youthfulness."

---

[5] That number is now close to twelve thousand employees.

EXERCISE: EVALUATING YOUR SYSTEM

In the above case study you have seen a variety of systems, structure, skills, style and symbols that are essential to creating a culture of continuous improvement. Most of this book is about your team and what you and your team can do to improve performance. But, it is also true that some of your ability to perform is influenced by the nature of the larger system or culture in your organization.

What are some of those factors in the larger culture that need to change to optimize your ability to perform? Your coach or leader can pass these on to a "design team" that can work on these.

Identify Possible Improvement in the Organization's Culture

Drivers of the Culture	What Would We Change?	Why? What Difference Would it Make?
Systems of Information, Human Resources, etc.		
Structure of Teams, Departments, etc.		
Skills of Leaders and Team Members		

Style of Communications and Decision-making		
Symbols that Create Unity or Division		

CHAPTER 2

CHANGE MANAGEMENT: ACTION-LEARNING

Many of the methods of training and development are designed for the convenience of the trainer, not the learner. They often don't work well because they are contrary to how normal human adults learn.

Adults learn in much the same way as does the child learning to play the piano. A very small amount of knowledge, followed by practice, followed by praise will yield more results than long lectures or thick books. How we develop continuous improvement for teams and individuals should follow a cycle of action-learning.

The best methods and the best of intentions can easily fail unless we take into account how adults learn in our organizations. During World War II a process that has become known as Training Within Industry (TWI) and its component Job Instruction (JI) was developed and was then adopted by Toyota as it developed its system of production. For management development Toyota and other Japanese companies added the role of the *sensei* or coach. These methods are effective because they are consistent with action-learning that recognizes the reality of how adults learn.

Malcom Knowles who pioneered the field of adult learning identified the following principles as critical to adult learning:

- Adults are autonomous and self-directed. They need to be free to direct themselves. Their teachers must actively involve adult participants in the learning process and serve as facilitators for them. They must show participants how the learning experience will help them reach their goals.

- Adults have accumulated a foundation of life experiences and knowledge that may include work-related activities, family responsibilities, and previous education. They need to connect learning to this knowledge/experience base.

- Adults are goal-oriented. Instructors must show participants how this class will help them attain their goals.

- Adults are relevancy-oriented. They must see a reason for learning something. Learning has to be applicable to their work or other responsibilities to be of value to them.

- Adults are practical, focusing on the aspects of a lesson most useful to them in their work. They may not be interested in knowledge for its own sake. Instructors must tell participants explicitly how the lesson will be useful to them on the job.

- As do all learners, adults need to be shown respect. Instructors must acknowledge the wealth of experiences that adult participants bring to the classroom. These adults should be treated as equals in experience and knowledge and allowed to voice their opinions freely.

What has proven most effective is to apply this action learning model to team development. The eight steps illustrated here constitute a cycle of learning and continuous improvement. In many ways they correspond to the PDCA cycle of improvement. However, they are a bit more specific to the actions required for effective learning and incorporate the role of sensei or coach.

The steps illustrated in grey are primarily knowing/gaining knowledge steps. The steps in black are more experiential and have more impact on how the learner feels. Knowledge and emotions are equally important in gaining sustained change in individual behavior or in the culture of the organization. Too often our training methods focus more on knowing, and too little on the emotive aspect of learning which is more likely to occur from experience. Often we assume that "if they know, they will do" and this is a false assumption.

Action Learning Cycle

ACT — PLAN — DO — CHECK

1. A Case for Action
2. Gain Knowledge
3. Agree on New Behavior
4. Apply & Practice Behavior
5. Receive Feedback from Coach
6. Gain More Knowledge
7. More Practice
8. Positive Sr+ for Success

Cognitive/Knowing
Experiential/Emotive

1.   BUILD A CASE FOR ACTION:

The administrators of the hospital, clinic or home care system must develop a clear case for action. Why do we need to change? How will working as a team may my life better? How will it improve patient care?

As management embarks on a process of continuous improvement they need to point to competitors, best practices, financial benchmarks and the voice of the customers who are telling us that we need to improve. And, it helps to make clear that learning and practicing the new skills will be a component of everyone's appraisal process. In other words, it is the job of managers and coaches to make change matter!

2.   GAIN KNOWLEDGE:

Transferring knowledge is what most corporate trainers do best. It is what classrooms are best designed to accomplish. It is why we have books and websites. However, knowledge very often does not result in behavioral change. It is the difference between taking a history course in which knowledge acquisition is the goal in itself; as opposed to learning to play the guitar. The former is primarily about cognition/knowledge, the latter is about habits or changes in behavior gained through experience and feelings of comfort with that new behavior.

If we are training teams to solve problems effectively, knowing the steps in a problem-solving model is important, but it is only the beginning of employing that knowledge for continuous improvement. Knowledge without action will not change habits or culture.

3.   AGREE ON NEW BEHAVIOR:

Intention is the beginning of change. The guitar instructor may teach a chord position or scale on the fret board. By itself, that is useless knowledge. It only becomes useful when practiced. The student must agree to practice the chords or scales.

What can a team in the hospital do to immediately start solving problems together? How can they quickly initiate action steps to improve hospital cleanliness or reduce wait times for patients? Doing something and measuring the outcome is when learning is most likely to occur.

The way I have designed this training manual is so that each chapter, beginning with Part One, is a training module and each training module corresponds to a deliverable – a desired performance or behavior. For example, the fourth chapter is on writing the team's charter. The deliverable or action step is to write their charter and gain approval of the sponsoring manager. Another chapter is on defining customer requirements. Of course, the team then brainstorms customer requirements, interviews customers, and agrees on customer requirements. So, each bit of knowledge and training then asks for a new behavior to be performed the team agrees on the behavior and then takes action.

4.   APPLY & PRACTICE NEW BEHAVIOR:

Imagine learning to play a musical instrument. How much knowledge of the keyboard or fret board is useful without then putting your hands on the instrument and practicing? The answer is very little. The important learning comes from playing the instrument, hearing the sounds, trying out different positions and chords and experiencing their difference. At one point I had the idea that I would learn to play the banjo and I bought a lesson book by Pete Seeger. When asked how often you should practice his answer was "Never. Just play!" What he understood was that the learning will come from the joy of playing, not from doing exercises or turning the experience into a painful task.

Practicing, evaluating, improving becomes a way of life. A Fast Company article (6/2/2009) on Toyota's Georgetown, KY plant described the reflection of one worker in the plant: "Artrip has been at Georgetown for 19 years. The way he does his work is so compelling it has become part of his personal life. 'When I'm mowing the grass, I'm thinking about the best way to do it. I'm trying different turns to see if I can do it faster,' he says." This is a clear sign that continuous improvement has become ingrained in the culture.

5.   RECEIVE FEEDBACK FROM COACH:

The role of the sensei has become understood as an element of Toyota culture. A sensei is, essentially, a personal coach and mentor. Someone who can guide, observes, and gives feedback and encouragement. It is worth noting that in every sport, whether the emphasis is on team performance or individual performance, there is always a coach. And coaches are not reserved for children or new learners. The best professional quarterbacks, tennis stars, professional golfers and opera singers all have personal coaches even though they are at the top of their game.

In a May, 2004 Harvard Business Review article (Learning to Lead at Toyota) Steven J. Spear does an excellent job of describing how a new manager is hired and trained at Toyota. His coach introduces him to the organization with structured observation and debriefing on what he sees. He is asked to find improvements, many each day, just from observing.

Then he is asked to work on the line with an assembly team. He is asked to find improvements and work with the team implementing them. He is then taken to Japan to again work with a frontline team and implement improvements, even in the very plant where the Toyota Production System began its development. At each step the sensei is encouraging him, guiding, and debriefing with him on the lessons he is learning. It is intensely personal and direct training and coaching. But, the sensei does little instructing in the traditional sense. Rather, he is creating experiences, asking questions, encouraging reflection.

Now consider how you develop teams in your own organization. Do they have a coach? Do they follow a structured learning process? Do they receive guidance, encouragement and feedback from a coach? Let me suggest that this is a necessity for the development of teams at every level of the organization.

6.   GAIN MORE KNOWLEDGE:

And now, the cycle becomes obvious. After each lesson learned, action or deliverable completed, the team receives feedback from the coach and then goes on to learn the next element of development: how to develop a balanced scorecard; how to map their work process; how to recognize variances of common versus special cause; how to reduce waste and cycle time, etc. And again this leads to practicing those skills.

7.   MORE PRACTICE:

The team and their coach should map out a series of ten to twenty steps that the team or individual will learn then do, then gain feedback and reflection. These steps should be those that lead to the complete set of behaviors you want a team to perform.

8.   POSITIVE REINFORCEMENT FROM COACH AND THE NATURAL ENVIRONMENT:

As teams practice the skills of continuous improvement they begin to have an impact on actual performance. They should be able to see this impact on measured performance, on graphs. This is in itself, positive reinforcement and strengthens the learned behavior. It is the job of both the coach and the manager to assure that new skills and desired behavior lead to good outcomes for both individuals and teams. These outcomes can be as simple a certification that you are a High Performing Team, or the opportunity to present the results of your efforts to senior managers. There are a hundred ways to "make it matter" to strengthen the behavior of continuous improvement and this reinforcement should be part of the designed learning process.

While there is nothing entirely new about the eight steps of this action-learning cycle, it is a key to establishing lean management and culture that is too often overlooked.

WHO TRAINS AND COACHES WHO?

Every organization today should develop internal expertise in continuous improvement because it is something that will be continuous, not a short term project. Develop your own cadre of coaches, rather than becoming consultant dependent. A consultant should help you develop your internal resources.

I have found it best to serve as the coach to a team of internal coaches who then use this workbook and other training resources to train every team of nurses, administrators, and support teams in the organization.

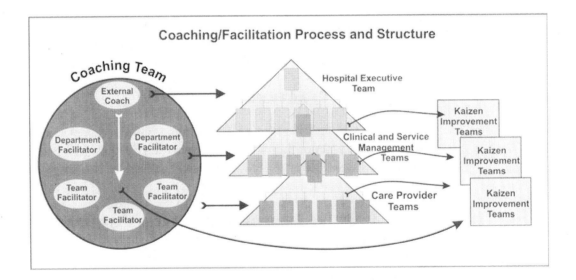

THE ROLE OF TEAM COACH:

- The coach will provide training in a sequence of modules that guide the teams through their development to becoming a high performance team.
- The coach will meet with the team leader to plan meetings and to provide feedback to the leader on her own leadership of the team.

- The coach will assist in customizing training modules and materials to best suit her teams.
- The coach will participate on a team of coaches who will evaluate the process of developing teams and work to improve that process.

THE QUALITIES AND COMPETENCIES OF A COACH:

- The coach should possess excellent communication skills, both the ability to present to small groups and the ability to effectively listen and provide feedback.
- The coach will be an effective team member herself.
- He will be well organized and able to plan meetings effectively.
- She will be respected by her peers for her ability to work well with others.
- He will be humble in his presentation, yet forthright and honest in his willingness to give his opinion on the progress of the group and its members.

LEARNING PLUS DOING: DELIVERABLES AND ACCOUNTABILITY

Continuous Improvement is not simply about learning. It is about doing and performing. It is about implementing a new culture in the organization. This workbook and associated training and coaching are designed to elicit new behavior on the part of manager and employee teams.

It is important that you manage the process of implementation. That means that there should be clear expectations in terms of what each team will do to implement continuous improvement. The following is a list of "deliverables," things that a team will do to demonstrate their learning and to improve their functioning as a team.

It will be helpful if the coach tracks the training modules completed and the deliverables completed for each team. This can be done on an Excel spreadsheet (contact the author for a copy). This will help motivate the team and keep them on track in their development.

The following twenty-eight items are auditable deliverables that are completed as a team progresses through their training. These action items are the implementation of the continuous improvement process for any given team.

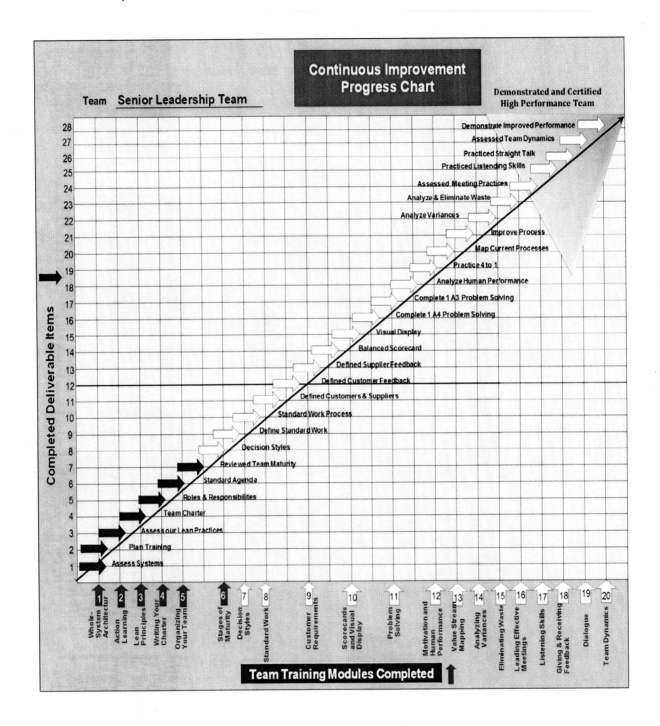

Key Deliverable to be Completed by Each Team	Related Chapter
1. Your team has considered the systems, structure, skills, style and symbols that impact your culture.	Chapter 1
2. You have met with your coach and agreed on a plan for training and doing.	Chapter 2
3. We have assessed how we practice the characteristics of lean organization and identified how we can move toward lean practices.	Chapter 3
4. We have developed a team charter that includes our SIPOC, principles and performance responsibilities.	Chapter 4
5. We have agreed on roles and responsibilities within our team.	Chapter 5
6. Our team has agreed on a standard agenda.	Chapter 5
7. We have identified ways to move our team to the next stage of maturity.	Chapter 6
8. The team has agreed which decisions will be command, consultative, or consensus decisions.	Chapter 7
9. We have defined standard work for members of our team.	Chapter 8
10. We have established a process to review conformance to standard work and to update standard work as we find improvements.	Chapter 8
11. The team has defined its customers and suppliers.	Chapter 9
12. The team has defined how it will receive periodic feedback from its customers.	Chapter 9
13. The team has agreed on a periodic process for providing	Chapter 9

feedback to its suppliers.	
14. The team has developed a balanced scorecard with process, customer satisfaction, financial and development measures.	Chapter 10
15. The team has posted graphs that are visual and up-to-date that reflects performance of the measures on its scorecard.	Chapter 10
16. The team has studied the PDCA (A4) problem-solving model and taken one problem completely through the problem-solving process.	Chapter 11
17. Team has implemented and demonstrated improvement in one of the measures using the A3 (DIMPABAC) problem-solving model.	Chapter 11
18. The team has analyzed a human performance issue and developed a plan for improving that performance.	Chapter 12
19. The team has agreed on, and implemented a plan to reinforce desired performance (practicing 4-1).	Chapter 12
20. The team has mapped one current process and found improvements in that process.	Chapter 13
21. The team has mapped the "ideal" or desired process for its key processes.	Chapter 13
22. The team has analyzed variation and identified causes of variation for its key performance measures.	Chapter 14
23. The team has analyzed its process to find waste, using the seven forms of waste as a guide.	Chapter 15
24. We have assessed our group process and identified ways to improve our meetings.	Chapter 16
25. The team members have practiced effective listening	Chapter 17

skills.	
26. The team members have practiced "straight-talk", effectively giving and receiving feedback.	Chapter 18
27. We have assessed our team dynamics and identified ways to build trust and confidence among team members.	Chapter 20
28. The key measures of performance are currently trending up, or are within ten percent of peak performance in the past year.	

Chapter 3

What is "Lean" & Continuous Improvement?

The purpose of this chapter is to present the basic principles, purpose and practices of lean management and for your team to begin the consider ways of applying the basic principles of lean to your area of responsibility.

Objectives:

1. Understand the over-arching purpose of Continuous Improvement and lean and how they may be applied to your organization.

2. Understand the synthesis of prior methods, theories and practices and how we are seeking to incorporate all of this learning as we implement a lean culture.

WHAT IS LEAN CULTURE?

Lean is a moving target because, at its heart, lean is a process of learning and improvement. It cannot be defined as something that is standing still or fixed. It is not simply mimicking what happened at Toyota or anywhere else. And, most importantly, it is not a kaizen event, a project, or something done by a consultant.

The short answer to "what is lean?" is simply that lean is the generic application of the Toyota Production System (or The Honda Way). It is not one thing but a set of things that are best captured as a philosophy rather than as particular method or technique. If you don't have the philosophy, you don't get it.

Here are some ways of describing lean philosophy or culture:

- Lean is a culture of continuous improvement practiced at every level of the organization and by every team.

- Lean is the application of the scientific method of experimentation and study of work processes and systems to find improvements.

- Lean is respect for people. It is respect for the voice of the customer and it is respect for those who do the work, who are "on-the-spot" and are, therefore, the "world's greatest experts" in their work.

- Lean is the elimination of waste in all its forms. Lean is the ability to distinguish between work that actually adds value to your customers and work that does not. By eliminating waste, you free resources to devote to value-adding activity that serves your customers.

- Lean is a work environment that assures the quality and safety of all work for both customers and staff.

- Lean is a focus on improving the work process and not on blaming people or creating fear.

- Lean is a culture of teamwork, shared responsibility and ownership that cuts through organization walls or silos.

- Lean is a culture that returns the joy to work. Honda speaks of the three joys of buying, selling and making the product. We do our best work when we have joy in our work.

- Lean is flow. Lean is an interruption free process that flows from beginning to end without interruption.

Now do an exercise with your team. Take each of these principles and identify how they are currently being practiced in your area of work and how they could be applied in the future.

When you do this, you will understand the purpose of everything else that will follow in this workbook and in the work of your team.

Lean Characteristics	How Do We Practice this Today?	How Could We Practice this Tomorrow?
Continuous Improvement		
Experimentation		
Respect for People		
Elimination of Waste		
Assure Quality and Safety, First!		
Blame the Process, Not People		
A Culture of Teamwork		
Joy at Work		
Interruption Free Flow		

A Brief History of Work Organizations

You may think your organization or industry is unique. And, in some respects you are probably right. But, you may be surprised at the degree to which the organization structure, systems, culture and processes has followed the same path followed by factories, education, and other work systems.

All work systems historically began with small organizations, much like the family farm and small craft shops. It evolved to big organizations with bureaucracies and the loss of intimacy that was felt in earlier days.

At the heart of lean culture is the small team seeking serve their customers in better ways. There is nothing new about small groups of people taking responsibility for performance. In fact, it is the most ancient form of organization, the origin of business. For thousands of years the work place was the home, and the work revolved around the home. The original corporation was not some impersonal legal entity with distant owners. It was the family, the family farm or small craft shop.

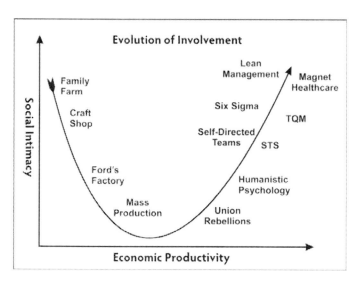

In the beginning, the people who did the work owned the work. It was their responsibility to think about their methods and the quality of their product, and they directly spoke with their customers. This direct contact and direct responsibility, along with the natural consequences of wealth or poverty, assured the motivation of those who did the work and their concern for customer satisfaction.

Family farms and craft shops used what we would now regard as highly inefficient methods. They had little technology, few economies of scale, and little opportunity for training and development or sharing best practices. The productivity, output per unit of input, was low. Bushels of corn per working hour, compared to any modern farm were horribly low. Therefore, the cost of food or goods was high and relative wealth low.

With the development of the combine and tractor, productivity increased, and the need for labor decreased. Workers moved from the rural family structure to the organized, specialized, structure of the cities and factories. In the last quarter of the nineteenth century and the first quarter of the twentieth century, every business learned the value of two things: economies of scale, or "mass production" and the application of the scientific method, or industrial engineering. These two methods, both of which increased productivity, also destroyed intimacy, the social relationships between employees and with their customer.

The same was true in healthcare. The doctor in the small town had little access to resources, information, and technology and could see relatively few patients each day. The efficiency of healthcare organizations has increased dramatically. But, in that gain of efficiency, something may have been lost. We may have lost that feeling of intimacy between doctor and patient and the intimacy between colleagues.

In the craft shop, the worker making a piece of furniture would sign his name to his work, like a personalized piece of art. Workers on the family farm and craft shop did "whole" work. They made a whole piece of furniture, a whole chair, not just a leg, a seat or a back to be assembled elsewhere. The social aspect of the craft and family farm system was unnoticed and not understood, but it was just as important as any economic understanding. It kept the family together. It united workers, management and customers. Once this was broken it would take a hundred years to repair.

The key element of the mass production system was the simplification of the work into standardized tasks, long production runs of standardized parts, and the close supervision of each worker so he would conform to the exact motions and speed defined by the new class of managers and supervisors. With this tight supervision and simplified work, there was no need for multi-skilled workers. This created the great divide between management and labor, thinker and worker, salaried and hourly.

This creation of division, a class system in the organization, was the beginning of a cancer that would eat at the culture for a hundred years. Hospitals would not be exempt from this same disease.

The first industrialist to make full use of this system was Henry Ford. Initially it took 14 hours to assemble a Model T car. By improving his mass production methods, Ford reduced this to 1 hour 33 minutes. This lowered the overall cost of each car and enabled Ford to undercut the price of other cars on the market. Between 1908 and 1916 the selling price of the Model T fell from $1,000 to $360. Following the success of Ford's low-priced cars, other companies began introducing mass production methods to produce cheaper goods. This changed the fundamental theory by which every organization was managed.

Frederick Taylor, the father of industrial engineering, developed the system of work standards and measurements to continuously improve the efficiency of mass production. Taylor's methods that emphasized the definition of one "right way" to perform a job led to a top-down rigidity that prohibited worker input to decision-making. It was the lack of moderation in the application of these methods that contributed to dehumanizing the workplace and a counter reaction. During the early part of this century, the workplace gained efficiency at the cost of intimacy and individual initiative.

One counter reaction to the industrial system of Taylor and Ford was the rise of the union movement, a rebellion not just for wages, but for dignity, a voice, a recognition that the human beings employed in the factory were not just subjects of engineering.

Managers would claim that there was a "union problem," but the real problem wasn't the unions; it was the system that produced them, a system that was, after thousands of years in which people worked in the family structure, a completely unnatural system, one that denied the basic human need for self-worth and self-control. When workers went down to the union hall, they called each other "brother" and "sister" and called for solidarity, brotherhood, and unity. They were calling for those things that had been taken away, the feelings of the family farm.

The development of humanistic psychology and its applications in organization development were a response to the alienation that had developed between management and workers. The field of organization development (OD) emerged primarily from the work of social psychologists. Social psychology focused on human needs, feelings, and the dynamics between people in groups. Researchers and writers such as Kurt Lewin and Carl Rogers developed models to describe the interaction within groups and the patterns of communication between individuals. During World War II the need to increase the rate of creativity led to research on group behavior and how best to increase the flow of ideas. What we now call "brainstorming" and other group techniques resulted from this effort.

In the 1940's Abraham Maslow defined seven stages of human motivation or needs.[6] This structure was useful in helping managers understand the significance of motivational influences beyond the simple need for survival and money. Maslow's work and the work of Herzberg[7] and McGregor[8] further developed the understanding of the relationship between organizational systems, management styles (Theory X and Theory Y), and employee motivation. This work became the foundation upon which numerous management and organization development practices were built. Job enrichment[9], Blake and Mouton's Managerial Grid, and various forms of group training and team building all have their foundation in the principles and values promoted by social and humanistic psychology.

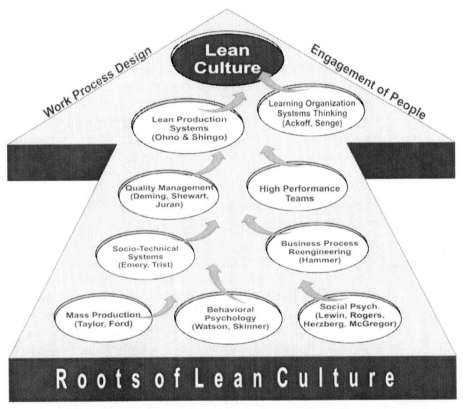

The development of Quality Circles in Japan can be traced back to the research in group dynamics and decision-making conducted in the 1950s in the United States. The quality movement was founded on the convergence of two disciplines, the discipline of group problem-solving and that of statistical process control.

6 Maslow, Abraham. "A Theory of Motivation." Psychological Review, 50, 1943, pp. 370-396.

7 Herzberg, Frederick. *Work and the Nature of Man*. World Publishing Company, 1966.

8 McGregor, Douglas M. *The Human Side of Enterprise*. New York: McGraw-Hill Book Company, Inc. 1960.

9 Meyer, M. Scott. *Every Employee A Manager*. New York: McGraw-Hill Book Company. 1970.

After World War II several Americans were invited to Japan to assist in the rebuilding of Japanese industry. Their teachings, filtered through the prism of Japanese culture, led to modern ***total quality management***. Among these teachers were W. Edwards Deming, Walter A. Shewhart and Joseph Juran. Shewhart's *Economic Control of Quality of Manufactured Products*[10] may be the most important book on quality or manufacturing ever written, and the seminars of these three fathers of modern quality management created much of the foundation of what is now regarded as lean management.

From Dr. Deming and Dr. Juran we learned to place the emphasis on performance to customer requirements, to define performance in terms of customer satisfaction, and to provide feedback to suppliers.[11] Dr. Deming and his disciples emphasized the importance of variability in process and of gaining statistical knowledge and control of the process. These views complemented the emphasis on teamwork and employee satisfaction that was emerging from the humanistic school of management.

Dr. Deming repeatedly emphasized the power of the system and the importance of managing the system. Unfortunately, Dr. Deming and the quality advocates provided no method for analyzing and changing the system of the organization. But, at the same time that Dr. Deming was becoming recognized in Japan, Eric Trist at the Tavistock Institute[12] in London began studying the environment of organizations and the interaction of the technical system of work and the social systems. The foundation study of ***socio-technical systems (STS) design*** was conducted by Trist in British coal mines. He found that the traditional culture of the mines was one of small, self-selected, and highly interdependent groups of workers, often members of the same family. When new technology was introduced into the mines, workers were assigned to single tasks controlled by external supervisors. The reactions of workers to this mass production culture were negative and led to high absenteeism, safety problems and low productivity. When workers were allowed to design their own organization, they duplicated their more traditional small self-managing work group. Productivity went up, safety problems and absenteeism went down.

What Trist did in coal mines was very simply to re-establish some of the patterns found in the family farm, combined with modern technology. This was a breakthrough. STS became the methodology for creation of a new organization in manufacturing plants, the self-managing, self-

---

[10] Shewhart, W.A. Economic Control of Quality of Manufactured Product. New York, D. Van Nostrand Company, Inc. 1931.

[11] Deming, W. Edwards. *Out of the Crisis*, Cambridge, MA, MIT Center for Advanced Engineering Studies, 1986.

[12] Trist, E., Higgins, C., Murray, H., & Pollock, A. *Organizational Choice.* London, Tavistock Institute, 1963.

directed, or high performing team. This proved so successful that it was adopted in all Proctor and Gamble plants. STS and TQM were operating in completely separate but parallel worlds, competing for management attention. Yet, there was an obvious synergy. TQM and Lean required the redesign of the work and organizational system. However, they had no systematic process to achieve that redesign. My colleagues and I combined these into what we termed "Whole System Architecture." This provided a methodology to redesign the system as Dr. Deming encouraged.

As the wave of Japanese automobiles became increasingly popular in the United States, closer examination of the system of production developed by Toyota led to increasing adoption of what we now call "lean manufacturing."

The evolution of production systems occurred in three stages (which have been well described in *The Machine That Changed the World*, the result of a five-year MIT comparative study of the global auto industry).[13] These stages are 1) craft production, 2) mass production, and 3) lean production.

The fathers of the Toyota Production System were Taiichi Ohno and Shigeo Shingo. Ohno was the production manager, later the Vice President, of Production at Toyota, while Shingo was the manufacturing engineer who is responsible for the development of many of the tools of what we now call "lean."

Shingo began his revolutionary work focusing on the die change process at Toyota, the key process in stamping metal parts. Large production lots were required because die change at Ford required 24 hours, by a separate group of workers, organized in a separate department, with separate managers and supervisors. For many years Shingo worked at speeding die change. But, the truth is that Shingo did not know how to speed the die change process. What he did was to ask questions and challenge the workers who were on-the-spot. It was these front-line workers, given encouragement, challenge, feedback and support to experiment, who made the breakthroughs. This process is important. Eventually die change was accomplished in minutes rather than days.

In accomplishing this quick die change, which became known as SMED (Single Minute Exchange of Dies), Ohno and Shingo had established a pattern that would be replicated throughout the factory. Small groups of workers would be treated as full partners in the process, responsible for their own work, able to improve and modify their process, and having

---

[13] Womack, James P., Jones, Daniel T., & Roos, Daniel. *The Machine That Changed The World*, New York, Rawson Associates, 1990

knowledge of the previous and next stages of production (their internal customers and suppliers) so that they would understand the requirements and effect of their work. Ohno found that these work groups, given the necessary information, worked to continuously improve their work process. This became the cultural assumption at Toyota, and it was entirely different than the cultural assumptions prevalent in traditional factories. This difference in culture is the primary explanation for the rise of Japanese automobile companies and the decline of the U.S. auto industry.

If you understand what Shingo did, you will understand that this exact same process can be applied within a hospital or any other organization. It is more about human nature that it is about the nature of a stamping press.

On the assembly line, Ohno formed workers into teams with a working team leader rather than a foreman. Teams were given a set of assembly steps and told to work together to devise the best possible ways to accomplish the assembly. The team leader would participate in the work, stepping in to help where needed. These teams soon accepted responsibility for housekeeping, small machine repair, maintenance, and checking their own quality. The teams would meet periodically to find ways to continuously improve (Kaizen) their process.

The total system in the Japanese plants became distinctly different than those in American auto plants. Lots were small, and quick change-to-order was a priority. They achieved the combination of efficiency and small production runs which American producers assumed to be contradictory. This was accomplished only by completely redefining the system of work and worker responsibility.

The task now for all managers is to combine the best of all the improvement efforts, to renew the human bonds and sense of responsibility that was present on the family farm without eliminating any of the efficiencies of lean production. *This is the purpose the Continuous Improvement.*

Continuous improvement begins with an assumption about human nature. That assumption is that when given responsibility, when given the facts, when given a way of keeping score and making decisions, the overwhelming majority of individuals will rise to the occasion and accept responsibility to improve performance. This is a truth about human nature whether it is in a factory, a hospital or a not for profit organization.

The philosophy underlying lean management and organizations is that we must respect the expertise and good intentions of all of our staff.

And, when working together in teams they will create collective wisdom and take collective responsibility for continuously improving the process, product, or service.

There is an important principle of philosophy underlying lean and continuous improvement. It is the principle of unity - unity between hourly and salaried; between customers and suppliers; unity between departments, functions, staff and operations. We all win together, we all lose together. It is the job of leaders to instill unity of energy and effort among those we lead.

The distinction between those who manage and those who do "work" is not useful anymore and will gradually be eliminated; it divides and de-motivates. But our structures and systems, our practices of management, have preserve the dead carcass of that system and hold back the gains that come when people are working as one body.

PART ONE
GETTING ORGANIZED

Continuous Improvement

CHAPTER 4

YOUR TEAM'S CHARTER

The purpose of this chapter is to help team members reach agreement on their purpose as a team and the principles that will guide their behavior. Your Charter will define your responsibilities and relationships.

OBJECTIVES

1. To engage the team in a discussion about why they are a team and their responsibilities as a team.

2. To have the team develop a charter that will define their work and responsibility as they serve their customers.

3. To have the team establish a code of conduct, or principles to live by.

WRITING A TEAM CHARTER

Your team should have a clearly defined charter that clarifies their boundaries and responsibilities. Every team has boundaries. No team (including the Chief Executive's team) can do anything it wants. Every team has a field of action and boundaries that define that field.

Developing the team charter should be done when a team is first formed. It should be jointly developed by the team itself and the team or manager to whom the team is responsible. One of the advantages of developing a charter comes from the conversation itself. Team members need to have this conversation so they develop a shared understanding their relationship, their commitments to each other, and their responsibilities as a team.

The following are the seven components that may be in a team charter:

1. Statement of Purpose: Why do we exist as a team?

2. Process Responsibility: What is the definition of the process that this team "owns" and is responsible for measuring and improving?

3. Process Boundaries: Where does this process begin, and where does it end? Who hands off stuff to us, and to whom do we hand off our finished stuff?

4. Principles: How will we behave toward one another? What is our agreed upon code of conduct?

5. Communication Responsibility to Managers, Customers, Customers, Suppliers and Other Teams: Whom should we keep informed and about what? From whom do we get feedback, and to whom do we give feedback? What information do we need to provide to a manager, and when?

6. Performance Responsibilities: What are the primary measures of performance for which we are responsible? This should not define specific measures (we will do that later), but the general categories of performance.

7. Membership and Sponsorship: What positions or functions serve as members of this team? Who gives us the authority to take action, make decisions, and to whom do we report?

DEFINING YOUR TEAM'S PURPOSE

Individuals have a personal need to find their purpose and to create their own energy source; they may find it in their faith, family or career. Teams are structured around a common purpose and manage their work to be of service to their customers, those who care about their work. Purpose may be found in genuine caring for those you serve and your fellow team members. The purpose of a larger organization should be found in its statement of mission and strategy. Why does the company exist? What will it contribute to the world at large, its customers, shareholders, and employees?

THE HIERARCHY OF PURPOSE

There is a hierarchy of purpose from the eternal to the instant, from the spiritual to the material. We can visualize this as a pyramid. At the top

of the pyramid is our largest understanding of our existence. Most of us gain understanding of our purpose from our religion or our parents. The concept of purpose is a spiritual concept. It is not merely intellectual, and it is certainly not material.

Many people have great difficulty relating spiritual purpose to their daily work-life. Yet, merely struggling with the question of how my work fulfills my spiritual purpose is, in itself, a step forward. Spiritual progress always comes from the internal struggle to resolve questions. If one has no questions, one has no spiritual progress. By asking this question we are seeking connection; we are seeking meaning; we are seeking unity between our spiritual and material lives; we are seeking an integrated life. Job satisfaction is in part a function of how we understand our personal and organization's purpose.

This is the first subject your team should decide together. Why do you exist, as a team? Who cares about the work you do? How can you have a positive influence on others?

1. How might this team contribute to my meeting my own purpose as an individual?

_____

_____

_____

2. Who are this team's primary customers, those who make use of and care about the work we do? Where does our work go, and why is it important?

_____

_____

_____

3. How do we contribute to the larger goals and purpose of our organization?

_____

_____

_____

4. What influence do we have on our community? Do we fulfill any purpose that is related to the needs and requirements of the community?

_____

_____

_____

Now, consult together with the members of your team. Use a flip chart and make a page for each of the four questions above. Have each member of your team go to the wall, and write down the most important answer they developed individually for each of these questions. Now discuss each of them. From the list that was put up by all of the team members, which items stand out as the most important and motivating answers. Feel free to combine and consolidate the answers.

From the consolidated list that is on the wall, discuss which answers represent the most important purpose of your team. Select three to five sentences that best define the purpose of your team. These answers should be motivating to you, and they should create a unity of effort on the part of all team members.

Our most significant purpose is...

_____

_____

_____

_____

DEFINING OUR CORE WORK PROCESSES

The work of teams is to manage and improve their work process. The charter should define what processes you "own."

It is important that the team take time at this point to define the basic landscape within which it works. For every team there are inputs and outputs. Someone or some group supplies the team with what it needs to do its work and someone receives its work.

Every team adds value by transforming input to output. It is the team's processes that achieve this transformation. In other words, if your team is a restaurant team, you receive raw food as input. You slice and dice, mix and stir, cook and prepare the food for serving. That is a process that adds value. You serve the food to customers who receive your output and are willing to pay for the value that you have added to the raw input. Almost every team does something similar, although perhaps more complicated than this restaurant team.

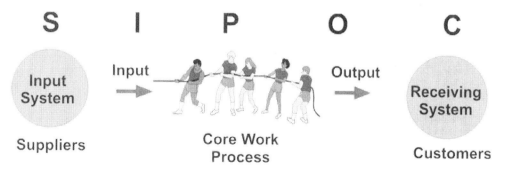

This flow, from input to output, is typically described as the team's SIPOC: Suppliers, Input, Process, Output, and Customers. In later chapters we will analyze these elements of the system, particularly the work process, in much greater detail. But, for the purpose of defining your charter, it will be helpful at this stage to define the basic elements of your SIPOC and particularly the processes for which you are responsible.

My Team's SIPOC

Suppliers	Inputs	Core Work Process	Outputs	Customers

CREATING A STATEMENT OF TEAM PRINCIPLES

Most teams have found it helpful to agree on a set of guiding principles that is an agreement on how they will behave as a team. On an athletic team there will be agreements to attend practice every day and to be there on time. Agreements like these are agreements to respect each other's time, each other's right to have a voice and to be heard respectfully.

It is a little bit like rules of the road, such as slower cars drive in the right lane. Most people would agree that these traffic laws and "rules of the road," which may appear to limit our freedoms, actually allow us a greater degree of freedom. If there were no traffic laws, we would be driving very slowly to make sure no one was flying through the next street corner. We can travel in relative safety and ease because we all agree to adhere to some common rules of the road.

If you did the exercise in the previous chapter in which you looked at a best and worst case team, you can now use that to say "how do we want to behave as a team?" and develop a statement of principles from this.

If not, follow the questions below to arrive at a set of team principles by which you agree to live:

1. Describe the best team experience you ever had. How did people behave on this team that led to this good experience?

   _____

   _____

   _____

2. Describe the worst team experience you have ever had. How did people behave on this team that led to this experience?

   _____

   _____

   _____

3. What role did the team leader, or facilitator, play that contributed to the good performance of the team?

    _____

    _____

    _____

4. Place two flip charts on the wall. Label one of them "Best Team"; and the other one "Worst Team." Now have each team member share the behavior that was characteristics of best and worst team experiences.

5. Now, discuss the two lists and from them, make a third list. This list could be labeled "How We Agree to Behave;" or, "Our Team Principles." Ask the group to reach consensus on the five to ten key behaviors that lead to successful teamwork.

    _____

    _____

    _____

    _____

So, now what do you do with this list of team principles, and the statement of purpose?

It is easy to put these aside and forget about them. This is almost a natural tendency as we dive into our daily work. Here are a couple suggestions that have proven to help teams live by their purpose and principles:

- Make a permanent flip chart, or some other kind of chart, that you can put on the wall each time your team meets. Just making these visible will serve as a reminder (like a traffic sign) and help the members of the team behave according to those principles.

- Sometimes the most subtle reminder is helpful. You may find that the team is in a heated discussion about some matter, and two or three members are interrupting each other, or two other members are carrying on their own conversation as if the group wasn't even there. The facilitator, or any member of the team, could stand up, go over to the list of principles, and just point at the principle that says, "We will listen respectfully, while others speak," or the one that says "We agree not to interrupt each other." The other members of the team will stop and take notice, and hopefully, bring their behavior into conformance with the principles.

- It is a very good idea for the team to periodically "process" how it is functioning as a team. Every fourth or fifth meeting, for example, your team leader might ask the group, "How do you think we are doing as a team?" The members can then look at the team's purpose and list of principles and ask themselves whether they are living up to their own agreements. If your team is like most teams, you will find that you are sometimes not living up to an agreement such as "Give every member an opportunity to be heard;" or, "Be sure to clarify our decisions and action agreements." This reminder will be both to the facilitator and the entire team. These gentle conversations are much better than anyone admonishing or punishing the team or its members. Remember that we are all learning how to function well in a team. This is just part of that process.

Here are some suggested items that might be among your principles.

- Arrive, start and finish on time
- Attend or send authorized backups to meetings
- Define clear purpose for meeting in advance
- Prepare and distribute agenda in advance
- Preview and assign order and time limits to agenda items at beginning of meeting
- Discuss critique from previous meeting
- Record assignments, decisions, date, and person responsible and issue in minutes
- Assign meeting roles: facilitator & timekeeper
- All participants assist meeting effectiveness
- Use positive decision-making techniques (such as consensus)
- No side bar discussions or interruptions
- Critique meeting effectiveness at conclusion
- Be prepared and participate

COMMUNICATION RESPONSIBILITIES

No team is an island and it has a responsibility to communicate its progress and problems to others. It is important to define to whom the team needs to communicate and how frequently.

You may find it helpful to fill in the following chart as you define your communication responsibilities:

To Whom Will We Communicate?	How Frequently?	What Information?

PERFORMANCE RESPONSIBILITIES

What are the primary measures of performance for which we are responsible? This should not define specific measures (we will do that later), but the general categories of performance and potential risks of failure.

MEMBERSHIP AND SPONSORSHIP

In many cases it is obvious who the team members will be. However, in many organizations there will be teams that include members who are permanently assigned to a different department, but who come together to provide a service or accomplish some other performance. For example in a manufacturing plant there may be a "technical operations" team made up of engineers, chemists and quality experts who work together with line manufacturing employees to manage technical aspects of the work.

Define the members of your team by position or function rather than by name. Over time, the names will change, while the team will continue to fulfill its purpose.

Also define the "sponsor," the position that will approve this charter and authorize the work of the team.

GAINING CHARTER APPROVAL

It is important that the sponsor, whether an individual or a team, review the charter and provide the team with any needed feedback. This "sign-off" will indicate ownership and commitment to the team by the leaders above.

CHAPTER 5

ORGANIZING YOUR TEAM

The purpose of this chapter is to develop the basic structure, roles and responsibilities on your team.

OBJECTIVES

1. To understand the role of different types of teams at that you may employ in your organization.

2. To understand what type of team you belong to and what that means for you.

3. To discuss and agree on the different roles on our team.

Let us assume that your team has just been formed. You have been given responsibility for a process, or set of processes. You know who the other team members are. Now, what do you do to turn this group of people into a genuine high performing team?

There are several things you need to do:

- First, define the different roles and responsibilities on the team.

- Second, clarify the roles or relationships with those who are connected to your team.

- Third, agree on your schedule of meetings, when, where and who.

- Fourth, create a standard agenda that you will modify for each meeting.

Different Types of Teams, Fulfilling Different Roles

Most organizations are a living organism. They change shape and structure and sometimes as they adapt to changing conditions and business challenges. Therefore, the structure of teams will change periodically. That is not a problem if everyone has learned the skills of teamwork and continuous improvement. They will take those skills with them as they join different teams.

Teams can be organized in more than one way, for more than one purpose. It is important to be clear which kind of team you are on. A team may be an on-going core work process team, an enabling or support team, a management or leadership team, or a kaizen improvement team that works on one specific problem.

Core Work Teams

These may also be called work cells, natural work team, self-directed teams, or teams in support areas like IT or HR. In a real sense they are the most important teams in the organization. They are teams that do the core work of your organization. Most organizations are a chain of core work teams that follow the flow of the process from input to output. Lean organizations have organized all front line employees into teams who take ownership of their work process.

Core Work Teams Follow the Process

But the structure of teams may not be as linear as the illustration above. For example you might be in the business of developing software solutions. You may have teams of software developers on three continents all doing similar work. Each of these areas may be organized into teams that are linked in their work. At the center is a management team. But, this organization may also recognize the need for learning and sharing knowledge across these teams, regardless of geography. There may be subject matter experts in a particular knowledge area such as graphical user interface. One of the triangles in the following diagram illustrates this team of subject matter experts. And, of course, there may be several other global knowledge teams of experts in other areas.

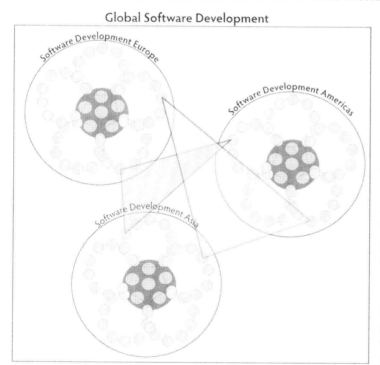

Global Software Development

At the center of each of these teams you can see the leadership team for that region. You can imagine that on this leadership team will be finance, human resources, information technology and others leaders responsible for other functions. It would also be logical to have these individuals serve jointly on a team for improving human resource practices, for example.

The basic idea of continuous improvement is that all levels of the organization are formed into teams that engage in continuous improvement of their work. These teams are linked together, with each team getting feedback from their customers, while management levels provide coordination and leadership to the teams. The goals, scorecards, and work of these teams are all linked together to create a unity of energy and effort.

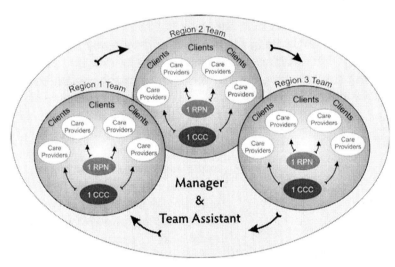

This illustration is of the client service teams designed for home health care delivery. You will see that there are several levels of teams. First there is the overall team led by a manager. Then there are geographic teams that are actually a cluster of sub-teams. The exact numbers of these teams will change as the process develops. But, you can see that everyone who serves customers is a member of a team and they will all participate in supporting one another, sharing information, solving problems and improving continuity and the quality of care delivered to their customers. They are all doing the core work of the organization.

This illustrates the more traditional assumption of work teams and management teams at each level. Everyone is on a team and the scorecards and objectives of these teams are all connected to one another.

Are teams ever entirely self-directed? No. We may use that term, but it never means that a team is actually without any management. Everyone reports to someone else and is accountable to someone else.

ENABLING OR SUPPORT TEAMS

In addition to the teams doing the core work there are critical support activities that enable the core work. Human resource management, technology services, quality management, financial support, and education are all essential activities. Just as it is beneficial for those in the core work to function well in teams, it is equally beneficial for those who work in these support groups to function well as teams.

This illustration is intended to describe the relationship between these enabling teams and core work teams. The specifics of the diagram are not important, simply the idea of how these teams overlap and interact with one another. We are used to thinking of units in an organization separated by solid lines. But that does not reflect reality. Where is "human resources?" Where is "information technology?" They are everywhere! Every team is dealing with human resources and information technology. How can you put these things into to isolated boxes?

LEADERSHIP TEAMS

Just as employees doing front line work should be a member of a team, every manager should also be a member of a team. The Board of Directors of a company is a team. The CEO and the senior business unit leaders are, or should be, a team. Each of these teams has responsibility for managing the on-going operations and that means that they are engaged in continuous improvement of operations. Their ability to collaborate, so solve problems and implement action plans, will all depend on how well they function together as a team.

It is also important that leadership or managing teams serve as a model for the culture, a model for the behavior that they wish to see throughout the organization. This is a key aspect of leadership.

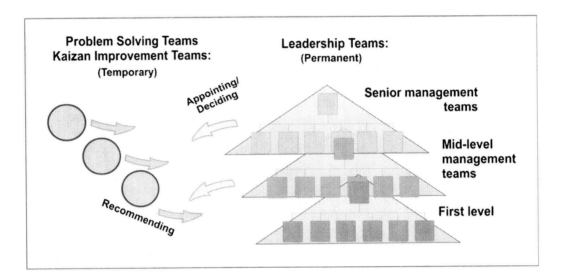

Just as core work teams have responsibilities for process improvement, leadership teams have this same responsibility. For example, there is a process of strategic planning. There is a budgeting and financial management process. There is a process for exploring new opportunities for products or services. Each of these processes is critical to the success of any organization. Studying and improving these processes is the work of leadership teams.

Too often executives and managers see themselves as "Lone Rangers" riding through the organization to find the bad guys and solve problems on their own. Many research studies have demonstrated that successful leaders are those who are successful at building a strong team around them, working well with that team, and giving credit to the team. In other words, they are good team leaders. The Lone Ranger was a mythical character, a figment of imagination. The idea that managers can ride into town and find the bad guys and then ride out of town is equally a myth.

KAIZEN, PROJECT IMPROVEMENT OR PROBLEM-SOLVING TEAMS

From time to time it is advantageous to put together a team comprised of members from different functions, different levels, or different regions of the organization to solve some problem or make improvement that cuts across many teams. Some problems cannot be solved within one core work team or one management team alone.

Kaizen teams are temporary. They are not the primary job of any member, but members who work on different teams will serve on a project team to find a solution to a particular problem.

Kaizen teams may be chosen to work on a problem by the management team, or permanent care delivery teams may identify a problem beyond their control and request that a problem-solving team be formed to attack that problem.

Unlike managing teams, these teams are not deciding teams, they are formed to study, analyze and develop recommendations that are then approved by a management team.

Which of the above types of teams do you belong to?

_____

What other teams does your team interact with in the organization? What kind of teams are these?

_____

_____

What are the key differences between your team and other types of teams in the organization?

_____

_____

MEMBER ROLES AND RESPONSIBILITIES

A baseball team or a work team succeeds because the players play their position with skill and enthusiasm. Outfielders, pitchers and infielders know their job, their particular contribution to the success of the team. On a team at work there are also distinct and important roles that need to be played.

When teams become mature and skilled it is common to rotate or share these roles. But first, we should understand the roles, practice them, and develop our skills. As we do, the performance of the entire team will improve.

THE FACILITATOR

Have you ever been in a meeting and sat there wondering just what the topic was and feeling like no one else knew either?

Have you been in a meeting when you felt that everyone was already in agreement, but people just kept talking and no one seemed able to just close the discussion?

Have you been in a meeting where a couple people did all the talking and others were never able to get a word in?

These are just some of the symptoms of poor facilitation that plague meetings. The ability to facilitate a meeting has nothing to do with rank in the organization. I have seen hourly employees on the shop floor do a fantastic job of facilitating a group and I have seen company presidents with virtually no ability to facilitate a meeting. Facilitation is a particular skill that can be learned by anyone, and someone on every team must be a skilled facilitator. Neither formal rank nor formal education guarantees that someone is a good facilitator.

What is facilitation? *To facilitate is to make something easy for others.* To facilitate a group is to help others in the group make their contribution. Facilitation can be as complicated as planning out an entire series of meetings or it can be the simple act of asking a member of the group if they would like to say something. But most of all, it is the concern for others, the sensitivity to recognize that some are talking so much that others are unable to express their opinions, or the sensitivity to recognize when the group has reached a point of agreement. It is the courage to bring order to what may be the chaos of conversation. It is the most frequent act of leadership that is most needed in organizations today.

And who is the facilitator? There is almost always someone who has the formal role of facilitation in a group. However, and this is extremely important, the actual act of facilitating, of making it easy for others to contribute, is something that every member of the group can and should do. Any member of the group can ask the question "Has everyone had an opportunity to give their opinion?" Or say "It feels like we are in agreement, are we ready to decide?" These are the types of facilitating questions or statements that "move things along" in a group and any member can help make it easy for others or the group to move along.

What is the function of the facilitator? It can be summarized in the following points.

Facilitation is...

- To create a clear agenda and help the group follow the agreed upon agenda.

- To state the topic and help the members of the group stay on the topic.

- To create an environment that is encouraging and safe for all to contribute.

- To help others contribute by inviting or encouraging them in a manner that is helpful to them.

- To be sure that all contributions are heard by the group.

- To bring topics to a close or decision when the need for dialogue or discussion is complete.

- To restate or clarify decisions in a manner that creates unity of understanding.

- To resolve conflicts that may arise in the group.

We are most likely to think of meetings led by the formal leader or manager of a group and assume that this formal leader will facilitate the group. This is the (F-L) Facilitator-Leader role. This is the way that most traditional meetings are facilitated. But, is there a rule that says that the formal manager must facilitate the meeting? Maybe it would be better in some circumstances for the formal manager to sit back, observe, and participate like other members. When the formal manager leads the discussion it is difficult for her to avoid biasing the group in a direction. The conversation is more likely to be open and creative when the facilitator is not the formal manager.

If it is clear that the formal manager of the group wishes to take charge or does not feel that the group is ready to take responsibility, this arrangement may be the best. It may also be the best in a development or training stage when the leader has the intention of modeling, demonstrating, good group leadership skills so others can learn.

It is often the case that the facilitator is not the formal leader or manager. It may be that a number of individuals on the team have been trained in the skills of leading meetings and the function of facilitation can be rotated among them. In some senior management teams where all

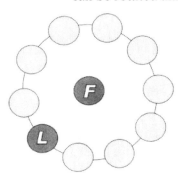

the senior managers had been trained in the team process and all were leaders of their next level teams the senior management may be happy to rotate the role of facilitator, or "chair" of the meeting, to a different person each month. Or, in some cases it is useful to have a facilitator who is not a permanent member of a team, but someone who is completely unbiased and is participating without any intention of contributing to substantive matters. If the group wants to discuss how it works together as a group, its internal process, it may be helpful to have an outside facilitator.

It is worth considering the different roles a facilitator may play in relation to the other members of the team. If a team is relatively inexperienced in the team process, it is likely that the team will be very dependent on the facilitator to make progress. In this case the facilitator plays a central role. However, as the team gains experience and maturity, the role of facilitation becomes increasingly less dominant and shared by other members of the team. In this case both the leader and facilitator may be pictured as part of the circle, but not in the center of the circle.

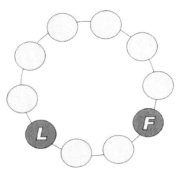

THE SCRIBE

It is very useful to have someone other than the facilitator designated as the "scribe" or note keeper of the group. This person will take minutes and distribute those minutes to all of the members of the group. It is helpful if the scribe has a laptop computer and composes the minutes during the meeting. At the end of the meeting he may read the decisions and action steps that were agreed to and check with the group to be sure that he has recorded them correctly. In many organizations the meeting room is connected with wireless Internet access and the scribe can email the minutes to the members of the team before leaving the room.

The nature of minutes is important. Some note keepers have a tendency to write down everything that is said, as if they were a court recorder. That is **not** what the scribe should do. In a team meeting the members should feel free to say things that are just ideas, and then change their mind as the dialogue progresses. If each comment is being recorded, this will create a hesitancy to offer ideas in a free manner and then to change one's position as new ideas are shared. The scribe should simply record the topics, the decisions, and the action steps that were agreed to.

The scribe may also maintain a "parking lot." A parking lot may be on a flipchart or in the minutes. This simply is a place to put things that we don't want to discuss now, but we should discuss at some later time. It is very normal for members of the group to think of things that are important, but, if discussed now, might take the group off their current topic.

THE TIMEKEEPER

It is usually assumed that the facilitator or chair of a meeting, who has her eye on the agenda, will take the responsibility of keeping the group on time. However, it is often the case that the facilitator is not a "pure" facilitator, but is an active member of the group, fully engaged in the conversation. In this case, it may be useful to have someone serve as the timekeeper.

If your meeting is planned for two hours, you may have five topics and each of these is allocated a planned amount of time by the group. It is very helpful if the timekeeper has his own flip chart. At the beginning of a topic, the timekeeper writes on the flip chart "30" if the topic has been allocated 30 minutes. With ten minutes to go, the timekeeper can get up and cross out "30" and write "10" on the flip chart without interrupting the conversation. He can do the same with five minutes and two minutes left. With two minutes left he might just stand by the flip chart, still without saying anything, but you can be sure that the group will be very conscious of the time. When time has run out, he then crosses off that last number of writes "0". At this point the facilitator will ask the group if this topic requires more time, and if so, does that mean they will extend the meeting longer, or take time from another topic. If your group has trouble getting through your agenda, you may find this method helpful.

SUBJECT MATTER EXPERTS (SME's)

Many teams have found it helpful to ask a member to specialize in some area of knowledge or some function, that is helpful to the group, but in which it is not necessary for every member to be involved. For example, there may be one person designated as the data management Subject Matter Expert (SME); this could be the member of the team who knows where to get the data for the team's scorecard. He or she will plot that data on graphs and report that data to the team at each team meeting.

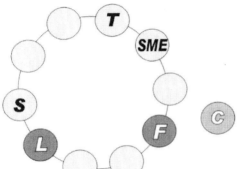

Another member of the group may take on the role of helping others with computers and software. In virtually every office there is a computer/software SME, informally recognized as "the person you go to" when you need help with your new computer or software. This person is acting as an SME, even though there may be no formal recognition of this role.

There can be an SME for communicating with customers and suppliers, one for training new members, or one for communicating with management or subordinates. It will be helpful to think about what regularly occurring tasks are important to the team and ask whether it will be helpful to ask a member to take on the role of SME for that task.

COACH

As teams are developing their skills, it is helpful to have a coach. For the same reasons an athlete benefits from the experience and skill of a coach, a management or work team can also benefit from coaching.

A coach is not a member of the team. It is very important that the coach not be from within the immediate "power structure" so that he is not hindered by concerns about being "politic" in his feedback to the team. A coach does not go out on the field and play. A coach is on the sidelines and observes the play, and from this perspective can give objective feedback. The coach may meet with the facilitator or leader before a meeting and ask for observations as to the progress and functioning of the team. The coach will then observe and may give the entire team feedback and may also meet with the leader or facilitator to give feedback on how performance of that role can be improved.

It is important that the coach be sensitive to the need to encourage the team, to provide positive feedback on the progress they are making. If the coach only gives feedback on areas in which the team can improve, his advice will soon not be welcomed. It is also important that the coach does not overwhelm the team with thirty things they need to do differently. No one, nor any group, works on thirty things at once. It is great if they work on two or three. Sometime later they can work on the others.

Coaches may be internal or external consultants who are hired to help with the process of developing the team's skills. When teams are senior management teams, it is desirable for the coaches to be external consultants who have both independence and extensive experience. However, with most teams, it is desirable to develop the internal capacity in the organization for an on-going coaching process.

Now it is time for you to define the roles on your team:

1. Who is the formal "leader" or "manager" of your team?

2. Who will facilitate your meetings? Is this a permanent assignment, or will this rotate among members?

3. Who will be the "scribe" or note taker for your team?

4. Who will be the timekeeper?

5. Are their subject matter experts who will attend your meetings? When?

6. Who will coach and provide feedback to your team?

SIMPLE THINGS THAT MAKE A DIFFERENCE

Sometimes very simple things can make a large difference in the success of a team and the effectiveness of meetings. The following are some issues you should check off to be sure you aren't overlooking these simple things.

It is very helpful if your team meetings develop a pattern, a recognizable "drum beat," easy to remember and easy to find. If the time and place of the meeting are constantly changing it is not realistic to expect the members to show up reliably.

Be sure that the place where you meet is quiet and a place that is least likely to be subject to interruptions. Hopefully, the room you meet in will be well lit, comfortable and have enough room. If the room is too small, it has a negative effect on the emotions of the group. It is important to have extra room for flip charts and for members of the group to stand up and cluster around a chart or other group exercise.

The room arrangement does matter. Look at the following possible seating arrangements for a team meeting. Note the position of the facilitator as well as the team members. Ask yourself the following questions about each of these arrangements:

- Which arrangement is likely to give the facilitator a greater sense of authority?

- Which will cause the members to defer to the facilitator?

- Which arrangement is likely to cause some members to feel more powerful than other members of the group?

- Which arrangement is likely to cause most of the member to feel comfortable contributing to the group?

- If you came into a meeting with each of these arrangements, where would you choose to sit?

- Which arrangement do you feel would be most conducive to reaching consensus? Why?

Choose a seating arrangement that reduces perceptions of unequal power if you want to encourage openness, sharing and the ability to reach consensus.

When planning a team meeting, you should think of any things you may need to use in the meeting. It is usually desirable to have two flip charts in the room, with tape to post pages on the walls (unless you have the self-sticking variety or walls with magnets). Be sure to have sufficient markers. And, you may wish to have "Post-it-notes" available for brainstorming activities.

When should team meetings be held? It is important to establish a regular schedule. In most work environments a weekly meeting is desirable. However, many teams these days are comprised of people who travel, live in different cities, or otherwise find it difficult to be in the same place at the same time. This may require a once a month meeting or virtual meetings.

Virtual meetings, either on the phone, or using some Internet meeting software or web site, are increasingly common. Regardless, establish a schedule that is predictable and at close enough intervals to provide for frequent review of your scorecard, solving problems promptly, and creating unity of effort among the team.

Let's make a plan for our meetings:

When and how often will our team meet?

_____

Where will our team meet?

_____

Which types of topics will we plan to discuss in virtual meetings (on the phone) and which will we reserve for face-to-face meetings?

_____

_____

Checklist of Simple Things

- ✓ Establish a "rhythm"

- ✓ Predictable place and time

- ✓ Interruption free Environment

- ✓ Arrange the Room for Maximum Participation

✓ Make Necessary Tools Available in Advance

✓ Plan Frequency for Short Interval Problem-solving

PLANNING THE AGENDA

The agenda is the plan, the roadmap for every meeting. Without a roadmap, a group can wander around looking lost for a long time. It is important to plan the agenda in advance and have the team quickly discuss and agree on the agenda as soon as the meeting begins. This gets everyone in agreement about where we are, where we are going, and how we are going to get there.

It is desirable to have the agenda visible. If meeting face-to-face this may be projected on a screen using an agenda template. However, it is not necessary to have it on a computer. It could be on a flip chart or on paper distributed to each member either before the meeting or when the meeting starts. Being able to visualize where we are in our progress is important to the comfort level of the group. As soon as members of a group begin to feel lost, they feel uncomfortable and anxious, and that may be expressed as frustration.

Here is a possible standard agenda that you might use as a starting point with a brief explanation of each item:

Standard Team Agenda

1. Approve/Agree on Agenda

2. Health and Safety

3. Recognition

4. Review action plans

5. Review Scorecard

6. Information sharing

7. Problem-solving

8. Action Planning

9. Next Agenda

10. Self-Critique

---

1. APPROVE/AGREE ON AGENDA:

This should also include agreeing on the amount of time required for each item. This should be quick. It is a common error that when a group starts discussing the agenda individuals want to start explaining why one item is important, and then someone replies to that, and quickly you are actually discussing the item, rather than agreeing that it is on the agenda. The facilitator needs to be active and maintain pretty tight control during this quick period of agreeing on the agenda.

If the agenda is somewhat complicated or will not follow an established pattern, the facilitator may wish to go to a flip chart and list the items for consideration as they are offered by the group. It will then be important to prioritize them. Simply ask the group if they can agree on the one or two most important items. You could ask "Which items are 'A' priorities?" You could then ask for "B's" or "C's" and the ask how much time will each require and construct the agenda starting with the highest priority items to be sure these are covered.

2. HEALTH AND SAFETY:

In any organization there are issues that are critical to the health and safety of team members. It is often a good idea to simply ask the question "are there any health or safety issues that we should discuss?" Or, "Does anyone have any health or safety tips they have learned or issues they have observed in the past week?" This opportunity to discuss these issues can bring healthy and safe behavior to the forefront the each team members mind and possibly prevent some unfortunate incident.

3. RECOGNITION:

It is part of our culture to focus on the problems, and most of us are pretty good at pointing out the errors, flaws and failings of our team members, management, family members and politicians. Pointing to our failures probably doesn't need to be on the agenda because it comes so naturally for most of us. Recognizing positive contributions is another matter. This does not come naturally to many of us, and it is a big factor in the motivation of the team.

We want to develop a culture of positive recognition. We are all here to serve our customers and it is very reasonable to assume that everyone is well intentioned. But, if we fail to recognize those good intentions and good behavior, the lack of appreciation can diminish those efforts.

Some teams, and often the higher you go in organizations the more true this is, there is a discomfort, anxiety, around offering recognition or praise. This is a good thing to overcome. It is a bad habit of a bad culture.

4. REVIEW ACTION PLANS:

One of the surest signs of poor team meetings is the failure to follow-up on action plans agreed to in previous meetings.

It is a good idea to record action plans either on an Excel spreadsheet or other electronic form and distribute it to all team members immediately after or during the meeting. Or, you can simply do it on paper. But, it is important that it be shared for all members to see and to take with them. The action plan from the last meeting should be displayed for all to see at the following meeting.

The facilitator simply goes through each item –the *What, Who,* and *When*, and asks "how did it go?" The person responsible for that item then reports that it was completed or gives some other explanation. If it was not completed, then the facilitator simply asks "What would we like to do about this now?" Generally the person who was responsible offers to get it done by a new date and the group either agrees that this is acceptable or comes up with another alternative.

This is accountability. However, it is a participative, shared, non-authoritarian accountability. When the group agrees to an action plan, they are acting together as the manager. This is "self-management," and it will have the effect of training the group members to follow through on their commitments to the team.

Here is an Action Planning form you can use. Electronic versions of this and other action planning forms are available from your coaches.

Action Plan			
Problem:			
Solution:			
Action-What?	**Who Will Act?**	**When?**	**Status**

5. REVIEW THE SCORECARD:

An important aspect of lean management is becoming a "scientist." When you develop a respect for the facts, the empirical evidence that something is working or not working, this leads you to gaining true knowledge. Watching your scorecard and graphing your data is the key to becoming a fact based team.

A team is a team because it keeps score. In a later chapter we will discuss the development of your balanced scorecard. A scorecard is useless unless it is reviewed regularly. Your scorecard should be reviewed regularly. It should be reviewed either weekly or monthly depending on your circumstance. Hopefully, your team will have identified the few key data variables that best reflect the performance of the team. These should be graphed, and the graphs should be on the wall for visual display at each team meeting. The review of the scorecard should include a discussion of "how are we doing?" on our measures. This should be a background for the team's problem-solving.

6. INFORMATION SHARING:

In most meetings there is a time for information sharing. For example your team lead may have information from funders that is important to pass on. Or there may be new health alerts or other information related to providing excellent care that can be passed on at this point in the meeting.

7. PROBLEM-SOLVING AND DECISION-MAKING:

This will often be the largest block of time in a meeting. This is when you dig into problems that have been identified while you were looking at your scorecard. How do we improve performance? What are the major constraints or problems in achieving your performance targets on your scorecard?

8. ACTION PLANNING:

Many meetings end with everyone in apparent agreement, yet nothing happens as a result. There is no action, no follow-up, and no accountability. The meeting begins in words and ends in words. The value of most meetings is not only in the sharing of information or discussion, but in the actions that follow. Too often we fail to make clear who is going to do what to whom, and when. Every meeting should end with a clear action plan, written down, with the names of individuals who are agreeing to act and dates by which they will act.

Use the action plan form given above or some other way to record your decisions to take action with the *What, Who* and *When* clearly stated.

9. PLAN NEXT AGENDA:

Every meeting should include at least a brief discussion of the next meeting's agenda. There are almost always items that are carried over, or individuals may express their desire for something to be placed on the agenda.

10. SELF-CRITIQUE

Lean management is about continuous improvement. Everything can be improved. We can all improve, every day. At the end of each meeting is desirable for the facilitator to simply as the question, "How did we do today?" Or, "What went well in our meeting today, or what could we improve?" This gives members the opportunity to make suggestions for improvements in a painless way. Without asking these questions members may have dissatisfactions that do not get aired until they reach some point of frustration. It is much wiser to seek continuous improvement than to wait for frustrations to rise.

Periodically the team might want to do a more in depth self-assessment based on their charter or their principles of how they work together, both of these documents can form the basis of a quick survey, ask your team coach for more details when you are ready to take this step.

The above items are suggested as a beginning point for your team to agree on a standard agenda. These items have worked for hundreds of teams, however; you should feel free to add other standard items you feel are important.

CHAPTER 6

STAGES OF TEAM DEVELOPMENT

The purpose of this chapter is to assist the team to recognize normal patterns of development or stages of maturity that most teams pass through.

OBJECTIVES:

1.   To recognize the characteristics of a mature and well-functioning team.

2.   To recognize the current level of maturity of your team.

3.   To identify specific ways that your team may advance to a higher level of maturity and performance.

As every team begins to develop its skills it will pass through stages of growth. Whether you are on a frontline work team or a leadership team you are likely to witness some behavior that you may at times find to be "adolescent" or which you may describe in some other way. It's OK! Just as your own offspring must go through some stages of exploration, testing, and learning to cooperate, teams go through very similar stages.

In 1965, Bruce Tuckman wrote that there are normal, even necessary stages of development that a team passes through as it matures. These stages - forming, storming, norming and performing - are often presented as if you MUST go through them as you must go through childhood and adolescence. It is true that there is a normal progression in the social development of a team, but there is nothing certain about these stages. In our work settings it is normal that teams members have already established some form of relationship, may have worked on other teams, and may go quickly and relatively painlessly toward maturity.

It is still a useful framework to consider your own development. Read through the description of these stages and then ask yourselves, "Where are we in this process?"

FORMING

In the first stages of team building, the *forming* of the team takes place. The team meets and learns about the opportunity and challenges, agrees on goals, and begins to tackle the tasks. Team members tend to behave quite independently. They may be motivated but are usually relatively uninformed of the issues and objectives of the team. Team members are usually on their best behavior but very focused on themselves. Mature team members begin to model appropriate behavior even at this early phase.

Leaders of the team may need to be directive during this phase.

The forming stage of any team is important because in this stage the members of the team get to know one another and make new friends. This is also a good opportunity to see how each member of the team works as an individual and how each responds to pressure. Trust is being established, and this will be the basis of their future work.

STORMING

Groups are then likely to enter the *storming* stage in which different ideas and individuals compete for consideration. The team addresses issues such as what problems they are supposed to solve, how they will function independently and together and what leadership model they will accept. Team members open up to each other and confront each other's ideas and perspectives.

In some cases *storming* can be resolved quickly. In others, the team never leaves this stage. The maturity of some team members usually determines whether the team will ever move out of this stage. Some team members will focus on minutiae to evade real issues.

The *storming* stage may be necessary to the growth of the team. It can be contentious, unpleasant and even painful to members of the team who are averse to conflict. Tolerance of each team member and their differences needs to be emphasized. Without tolerance and patience, the team will fail. This phase can become destructive to the team and will lower motivation if allowed to get out of control.

This is the stage during which coaching and facilitation may be most critical. The team and individuals may benefit from feedback by an objective third party.

NORMING

At some point, the team will likely enter the *norming* stage. Team members adjust their behavior to each other as they develop work habits that make teamwork seem more natural and fluid. Team members often work through this stage by agreeing on rules, values, professional behavior, shared methods, working tools and even taboos. During this phase, team members begin to trust each other. Motivation increases as the team gets more acquainted with the project or process for which the team is responsible.

Teams in this phase may lose their creativity if the norming behaviors become too strong and begin to stifle healthy dissent and the team begins to exhibit groupthink.

Leaders of the team during this phase tend to be participative more than in the earlier stages. The team members can be expected to take more responsibility for making decisions and for their professional behavior.

PERFORMING

Hopefully, your team will reach the *performing* stage. These high-performing teams are able to function as a unit as they find ways to get the job done smoothly and effectively without inappropriate conflict or the need for external supervision. Team members have become interdependent. By this time they are motivated and knowledgeable. The team members are now competent, autonomous and able to handle the decision-making process without supervision. Dissent is expected and allowed as long as it is expressed in an acceptable manner.

Leaders of the team during this phase are almost always participative. The facilitation of the team may now rotate among members. The team will make most of the necessary decisions. Even the most high-performing teams will revert to earlier stages in certain circumstances. Many long-standing teams will go through these cycles many times as they react to changing circumstances. For example, a change in leadership may cause the team to revert to *storming* as the new people challenge the existing norms and dynamics of the team.

In which stage is your team? What are some of the signs or behavior that indicates its stage of development?

_____

_____

What are some things you can do to help the team move through the current stage and get to the performing stage?

_____

_____

TEAM MATURITY AND DECISION-MAKING

Another way to understand the maturing of a team is to consider the degree to which the team takes responsibility for its own performance and how managers adjust to their maturity.

When a team acts as a truly high performing team, initiating action to communicate with customers, measuring its own performance, and acting with self-initiative to make improvements, it may be said to have high *performance initiative*. Many teams when they are first formed are waiting to be told what to do. They are looking to do what is acceptable, not to initiate improvements.

If you look at the next diagram, you will see a matrix with Performance Initiative on one axis. On the other axis is the control of decisions – who is making the decisions? An easy way to think of this is to think about a child growing into adolescence, and then into mature adulthood. Every parent has struggled with the issue of how much freedom to allow a teenager. Of course, every teenager wants more freedom to decide when to come home at night, whom to associate with, etc. How does the parent know when to let go and "delegate" these kinds of decisions to the young person? The answer lies in performance. The more maturely teenagers behave; the more reasonable it is to allow them to make their own decisions. The parent moves through a progression from telling, through advising, to delegating.

What happens if the parent gives up control of decision-making too soon? This can lead to poor performance. The teenager may not be ready to make his own decisions and may make unwise ones. Or, what happens if the teenager is ready to make her own decisions, but the parent is over-controlling? This is de-motivating to the young person and is likely to lead to rebellious behavior.

Teams are not that different. When teams take responsibility for their own performance, the manager should assert less control and delegate more. On the other hand, if the team fails to take ownership of its performance or fails to initiate improvement efforts, the manager has a responsibility to be more directive.

What sometimes happens when implementing teams is that the manager is told that he "is supposed to let go." So he does, even though he may be very uncomfortable and sometimes this discomfort is based on his rational observation of the team's behavior. His gut may have told him the truth, that the team was not ready to take responsibility on its own. If the manager let's go and the team is not ready, the result is likely to be poor performance. This is a common cause of failure. Of course, failure also occurs because of over-control and the subsequent de-motivation of the team.

A human life progresses from dependence through independence to interdependence. In other words an infant, when born, is entirely dependent on the parents. Human beings are one of the least independent of infants. Fish are more capable at birth. But, as the infant matures in childhood she gains degrees of independence, walking, feeding, and learning to dress herself. The primary characteristic of teenagers is their declaration of independence – "I can do it myself!" But, that is not yet maturity. When you enter marriage you enter an agreement to be interdependent. In maturity individuals, teams, even companies and countries recognize the need for close collaboration, mutual interests, and development of the behavior required for effective interdependence.

Interdependence *Adulthood*

Teams collaborate with customers, customers and other functional areas to make decisions that are in the best interest of all.

Independence *Adolescence*

The team exerts autonomy and begins to take control of performance. They act in the best interest of the team, but don't necessarily think about how the team's actions affect overall performance and do not involve "outsiders" to help make the best decisions.

Dependence *Childhood*

Members depend on managers to worry about the overall performance of the team. They are only concerned that they do *their* job well, and that their personal needs are met.

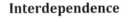

CHAPTER 7

CLARIFYING DECISION STYLES

The purpose of this chapter is to clarify who will make what decisions when, and in what style.

OBJECTIVES:

1. To clarify how our team will make decisions in different situations.

2. To understand situational decision-making styles – why different styles are effective in different situations.

3. To understand the relationship between decision-making styles and the culture of the organization.

As you build a lean culture it will be necessary to shift how decisions are made throughout your organization. You will increasingly become a high-trust culture as teams demonstrate their maturity and their ability to improve performance.

This is a normal transition as everyone learns to focus on the process, rather than blaming people, and everyone develops a unity of effort around providing the best possible care to customers.

The reality of most work teams is that each individual is making some decisions every day. We must trust in the responsible nature of employees who operate equipment, interact with customers or do other work on their own. Most work involves making decisions.

CLARIFY WHO MAKES WHAT DECISION AND HOW:

A true lean culture is one in which consensus decision-making is valued. The value of creating ownership for a decision and assuring that a decision is of the highest possible quality is more important than making it quickly.

One day I received a phone call from Scott Whitlock, who at that time was Executive Vice President at Honda America Manufacturing in Ohio. He was using a previous book I wrote to train new managers. He asked me, "How many do you need to achieve consensus?" I had no idea what he was talking about. In my book I had eight principles that Honda was trying to follow. One of them was *The Consensus Principle*.

I asked Scott, "What is the decision you are trying to achieve consensus on?" He replied that it was the drug policy. I was somewhat surprised at this. I then asked, "Well, how many people are you trying to involve in the consensus?" He replied, "Ten thousand. It's your principle!" I was astonished. Yes, it was my principle, but I never imagined that it would be applied to reach consensus among ten thousand employees on something like the drug policy. I then asked him, "Well how many are in agreement now?" He replied "Eighty-seven

Decision Style Distribution

The Crisis Exception

The Collaborative Majority

The Strategy, Process & Goals

Command   Consultative   Consensus

Who Knows, Who Cares, Who Must Act, When Must It Be Made?

percent." I thought that was pretty good. But, Scott didn't think it was enough. He said, "Well we don't think it is good enough. We are going to go around again."

Now imagine that he achieved a ninety-five percent consensus on the drug policy and every one of ten thousand employees had an opportunity to offer their input and agree or disagree. How difficult do you think it will be to implement that policy? Compare that to a company in which a few alleged experts write the policy and now managers have to instruct the employees and enforce discipline to that policy. Which do you think will have an easier time of it? It may be considered an unnecessary waste of time to involve ten thousand people in the decision process. But, then the time saved in implementing that policy may far outweigh that time.

WHO KNOWS? WHO CARES? WHO ACTS?

These three questions provide a good guide to who should be involved in making decisions. There is always a balance between gaining commitment and speed of decision-making. It is quick and easy to have one person make a decision. But, there is likely to be low commitment and lost knowledge by failing to engage those who know, who care, and who must act.

Too often an outside expert or an internal manager who thinks she or he knows best make decisions, but the decisions are not "owned" by those who must implement them. The implementation process then becomes one of constant selling, controlling, demanding and blaming. Taking the time to develop consensus, ownership by those *who know, who care,* and *who must act,* is almost always a wise investment.

Members of a team want to understand how decisions are made and who makes them. Many of the conflicts that arise around teams involve a failure to create this clarity. If team members think they are going to make a decision, and a manager then makes the decision alone, they will be upset even if they don't disagree with the decision. Disunity results from differing expectations and feeling betrayed that an agreement (real or imagined) isn't being followed.

In my own company we had a once a month team meeting when all of the consultants and administrative staff would meet for the day, share learning, discuss the company's finances, marketing, etc. More than once, I would put an issue before the group and ask for input. Frequently, one of the consultants would ask me, "Larry, are you asking us for input so you can make the decision, or are you asking us to reach a consensus and make the decision?" Good question. Sometimes I wasn't sure and needed to clarify this in my own mind. Several times, I asked them whether they thought I should make the decision or let the group reach a decision. On most of those occasions, they preferred that I make the decision after listening to their input. They didn't want to spend the time to reach a consensus. It is not true that team members want to be involved in making every decision, but they do want input, and they want to know how those decisions are made.

Here is a quick primer on assigning decision responsibility: Consider three types of decisions: Command, consultative and consensus. The criteria for deciding which to use are *who knows, who cares, who acts,* and *when must it be made?*

COMMAND DECISIONS

Command decisions are those made by an individual. Individual command authority is not dead and not merely a left over dinosaur of the Roman Legions. Of course, command worked well on the battlefield on which quick decisions were required and obedience won battles. Even today, if the building is burning down, if the machine is spitting smoke and oil, if the customer calls and is furious that he got the wrong material delivered – is the right answer to call a meeting? Definitely not! These are decisions in which speed is more important than reaching consensus. These decisions are best left to individuals who are on-the-spot and have expert knowledge.

Speed and expert knowledge are two reasons for command to be the preferred decision style. In the operating room, with the patient cut open and the cardiologist holding a heart in his hand that has just stopped beating – do you want him to call a meeting to get help through consensus decision-making? Not if it's your heart! Of course, you want him to use his expert knowledge and make a decision, fast! The greater the degree of knowledge an individual has compared to others on a team, the more likely a command decision is appropriate. The greater the required speed, the more likely it is that command decision-making is appropriate.

An organization in which command decision-making is predominant is an organization that lives in frequent crisis. This raises serious questions about the ability of the leaders to plan, engage in systematic action, and develop the people below them. Or, it is an organization dominated by personalities whose egos prevent them from letting go of decisions and trusting others. Predominance of command decision-making reflects low trust and will soon de-motivate employees.

CONSULTATIVE OR SHARED DECISIONS

Consultative decisions involve selective involvement by those who know, care, or must act. If a customer calls with a problem, they do not want to be told that you will put their problem on the agenda for your

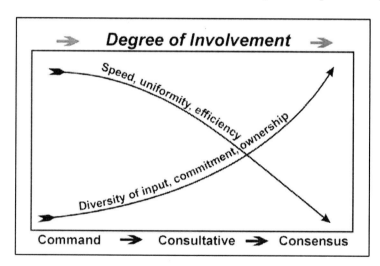

next team meeting! They need to know whether you can respond appropriately NOW! But, if you say, "I understand and I will contact my team immediately and get back to you within fifteen minutes to let you know how we will solve this problem" this will likely satisfy the customer. They will understand the need to consult others quickly. But, they must know that you are in control of the decision and you are taking responsibility.

This is consultative decision-making. Consultative decisions are those when an individual maintains responsibility for getting a decision made, but takes time to consult with those who know, who care, and who must act.

CONSENSUS DECISIONS

Consensus decisions are true team decisions where you turn over the decision to the group. But, let us be clear in our understanding of consensus. There is an academic understanding of consensus in which a topic is discussed until everyone has the same point of view. This can take forever! In the practical world of business time is essential and we have to get decisions made. We must employ what I will call *practical consensus.* Practical consensus is like democracy. You have the right to be heard, the need for others to listen, and then there is the obligation to let go of your personal point of view and sacrifice your view to the collective wisdom of the team. Let's review that because it is a critical understanding about consensus. *Practical consensus* requires the following:

- First, all members of the group have an obligation to honestly and frankly state their opinion and offer any facts they may have.
- Second, all members of the group have the duty to listen respectfully and consider the views of others. Each member of the group must have the opportunity to express his or her case for their preferred decision or course of action. And after you have been heard...
- Third, all members of the group have the obligation to achieve unity, to go along with the majority view of the group and act as if it were their own personal decision.

When do you do this? First, when the conditions of speed and individual expertise are not the most important factors. When the quality of the decision, commitment of the players, and unified action are most important, it is time to use consensus decision-making. Consensus decisions involve a cost – the cost of time, energy of the group, and the risk that you may not like the decision.

When do you employ consensus decision-making? For those decisions that involve long-term goals, and how we do things, our ongoing processes. All members of the group have an investment in the goals of the group and the "how" and "why" we do our work. Involvement in these types of decisions gains commitment, gains the wisdom of the group, and provides for shared learning.

Ask your team which decisions should be command, consultative or consensus. You can create a great deal of clarity and have the group focus on

Lean Organization
High Trust - High Commitment

The Crisis Exception | The Collaborative Majority | The Strategy, Process & Goals

Command | Consultative | Consensus

Many Know, Many Care, Many Must Act, Decisions Made for the Long Term.

those things that add most value for the group. The time and energy of teams is often wasted with trivial and inappropriate decisions. Use common sense.

EXERCISE: CLARIFY DECISION STYLES

Make a list of decisions that get made by your team. You might brainstorm this and make a list on a flip chart in a team meeting. Then look at the decision style criteria on the previous pages and make a list of which decisions should be command, which consultative, and which consensus. Also indicate who is involved in each:

1. Command Decisions:

_____

_____

_____

_____

2. Consultative Decisions:

_____

_____

_____

_____

3. Consensus Decisions:

_____

_____

_____

_____

CHAPTER 8

STANDARD WORK

The purpose of this chapter is to familiarize you with the concept of *Standard Work* and *Leader Standard Work* and give you an opportunity to define the standard work among your team members.

OBJECTIVES:

1. To define that work or behavior on the part of team members that should be standard, periodic, behavior that will support the performance of your team.

2. To establish those patterns of behavior that will not only assure the effectiveness of the team in meeting its objectives, but to assure that optimum care is provided to our customers.

One of the aspects of lean management that has been adopted from manufacturing, and has proven effective in many different settings, is the idea of standard work and leader standard work. The idea is very simple. You can imagine on an auto assembly line that a standard way is developed to accomplish the task of painting the body, or installing the engine or other component. These standard work procedures reduce error and reduce the need for "reinventing the wheel" over and over again.

Developing standard work should not be confused with making things rigid or bureaucratic. There is a balance between continuous improvement and standard work. Lean organizations are constantly seeking to improve the way they do things. Therefore the standard work changes as soon as someone or some team demonstrate a better way. In fact, Taichii Ohno, one of the founders of lean management said "Where there is no standard work, there can be no kaizen (continuous improvement)."

When we all know our standard work it can reduce misunderstandings and reduce errors when one person needs to step in to cover for another person.

To achieve a significant change in organization culture it is necessary to reconsider the work of all employees, at all levels. One of the most common mistakes made when implementing lean management is to assume that the change is one that must occur at the first level, and not at management levels. In fact, the changes at management levels are just as important as the changes at the first level. How managers think, act, set the example, and take personal responsibility for improvement, will determine the success of the organization.

WHAT IS STANDARD WORK?

One way to understand standard work is to think about your personal life or non-work activities. For example, when you are preparing a meal there is a standard way that you set the table. You do not have to spend time thinking about what utensils to put on the table or where they are placed because long ago you developed or accepted a standard way to set a table. When you start to prepare a meal that you have prepared many times before you have probably developed a standard way of preparing that meal. And, when you get up in the morning or go to bed at night, you most likely have standard things you do to prepare yourself for the day or the night. All of these are personal and informal standard work.

If you are assembly a product in a manufacturing facility, you do not reinvent how the product is assembled each day, nor do you have to reinvent the work of each employee. There may be some unique tasks each day, but the majority of the work tasks are standard.

Similarly, in a service organization, such as healthcare, much of the work has very significant consequences in terms of the health, safety and well-being of customers. In healthcare there has been a traditional culture of individual expertise and individual decision-making as to how to conduct procedures and how to assist customers. This is understandable when doctors each pride themselves on their expertise and do not want to be restricted or instructed as to how to do their work. But, freedom for everyone to decide has its price. There are standard therapies that have proven successful for different illnesses. There are standard practices such as washing hands or putting on antiseptic gloves before treating a patient. These habits serve the purpose of insuring quality and safety, just as similar standards do in a factory.

Standard work is also for team leaders, managers and even executives of the organization. The culture of management has often been one of feeling superior to the need for any routine or standard work. Yet, in fact, the CEO of an organization has standard meetings that he or she must attend, standard reports to review, and standard activities that support and encourage the work below. This is *leader standard work*.

Leader standard work typically does the following:

- It reviews standard work at the next level.
- It reviews the quality of performance and the conditions that impact performance.
- It considers the environment, cleanliness, and orderliness of the work environment.
- It includes a check on visual controls.
- It includes listening, learning, and seeking to understand.
- It incorporates the responsibility to motivate and encourage employees.
- It includes a focus on process, not just results.
- It documents the job of "lean management."

Leader standard work creates a disciplined process of management. If you are the coach of a professional football team, for example, it is important that your own behavior creates a model of disciplined action. You expect your players to eat properly, run a certain amount each day, and practice their routines and plays, in a disciplined manner. They are like the front line workers in an organization. By seeing that you adhere to a disciplined process of management yourself, this encourages them to do the same. Military officers understand this same principle. You cannot expect disciplined behavior in the front ranks if you don't demonstrate discipline yourself.

HOW MUCH TIME IS DEVOTED TO STANDARD WORK?

There is no one right answer to how much time should be devoted to standard work. However, it is logical to assume that at lower levels a higher percent of time is devoted to standard work and at higher levels a greater percent to unique work.

It is true that at more senior levels a greater majority of time is spent on unique activity, planning new business activity and solving larger problems. It is reasonable to assume that from the first level employee to the CEO there is a progression from more standard work to more unique work.

Position	% Time Devoted to Standard Work
Executive Management	5-15%
Middle Managers	15-25%
Plant Managers	20-40%
Department Managers	30-50%
Team Leaders	60-80%
Front line Employees	80-100%

DECIDING ON STANDARD WORK

Your team coach may be able to provide you with a list, form and categories of standard work that has been developed by other teams and other leadership teams. These are a good starting point for you to develop your own standard work.

In a manufacturing setting standard work for employees might include some or all of the following:

- Attend daily huddle before shift
- Receive daily production schedule
- Clean and order work area before shift
- Clean and order work area at end of shift
- Conduct start up preventive maintenance on equipment
- Monitor production rate
- Conduct scheduled preventive maintenance on equipment
- Complete production tracking sheets/reports
- Update charts of area work performance
- Conduct quality checks

Here are some categories of standard work that you might consider for a nurse or nursing team:

1   Client Visit
    a. Environmental scan for health and safety factors
    b. A script for standard introduction and questions.
    c. Standard practices as per body mechanics.
2   Planning and Communication with Customers and Funders:
    a. Periodic checking for communication from your Client Care Coordinator, customers or managers.
    b. Pre visit questions to ask.
    c. In visit charting and reporting.
    d. Initial progress reports.
    e. Post visit reporting and communication.
3   Team Member Activities
    a. Daily or Weekly team huddles
    b. Information sharing with your team
    c. Follow up on action items.

LEADER STANDARD

As you develop lean management practices standard work for leaders will become clearer and the usefulness of standard work will be demonstrated at the management levels of the organization.

It is important that your management think through the important tasks for each position. However, at each level the focus should be on helping, facilitating, encouraging, and supporting the work of the next level below. Ultimately it is the first level that does the most to serve the customers.

For one organization in the healthcare field, the following were some initial categories of leader standard work. You can use this as a beginning point for your own development of your leader standard work.

1. Observing Work Practices
    a. Observe KPI data on dashboard and visual display.
    b. Check to see that visual displays of key performance data are up-to-date.
    c. Periodic observation of care providers visits.
    d. Observe the standard work of the next level
    e. Provide feedback and recognition.
    f. See and reinforce improvement made by those doing the work.
2. Planning
    a. Plan weekly management meetings
    b. Budget review and budget planning
    c. Personnel resource planning
    d. Attend planning meetings
3. Reporting and Communicating Activities
    a. Review occurrence reports
    b. Reporting and liaison with funders
    c. KPI review meetings
    d. Town hall or other employee meetings
    e. Attend weekly management meetings
    f. Business plan and financial reviews.
4. Managing Others and Problem-solving
    a. Personal development plans
    b. Provide recognition.
    c. Assist others in problem-solving

The above categories are just a starting point or suggestions. It will be very useful for your team coach to assist you by sharing work developed by other teams or best practices from practice leaders in the organization.

The following pages present a worksheet that may be used in developing and maintaining leader standard work practices. This form would be developed for each level of work, including team members and senior managers.

Standard Work Worksheet

Position:

Name:

Date:

Tasks: Work Practices	Time of Day	Daily Completion	Weekly Completion	Monthly Completion

Notes: Actions & Improvements

Tasks: Observe Performance and Visual Display	Time of Day	Daily Completion	Weekly Completion	Monthly Completion

Notes: Actions & Improvements

Standard Work Worksheet

Position:

Name:

Date:

Tasks: Safety & Environmental	Time of Day	Daily Completion	Weekly Completion	Monthly Completion

Notes: Actions & Improvements

Tasks: Meetings and Problem Solving	Time of Day	Daily Completion	Weekly Completion	Monthly Completion

Notes: Actions & Improvements

CHAPTER 9

DEFINING CUSTOMER REQUIREMENTS

The purpose of this chapter is to help the team identify their customers and suppliers, know the requirements of their customers, and set broad goals to meet their customers' needs.

OBJECTIVES

1. To identify those for whom you work, your customers.

2. To identify the types of requirements of your customers.

3. To identify your suppliers and the type of feedback that would help them serve your team better.

4. To reach agreement with your team on your customers and suppliers.

Our success is directly related to the degree to which we understand and appreciate the needs and requirements of both our customers and of our funders. For many years the pursuit of quality in either products or services has focused on defining exactly what will please, even delight, those who are on the receiving end of those products or services. We often think we know, but often do not know exactly what it is that creates satisfaction among our customers. During this chapter your team should seek to achieve clarity on those requirements.

There is joy in work when it is done in the spirit of service to someone else. There is joy in work when you feel that you have control over the quality of your work. There is even more joy in work when you know that you are expert and that you are daily striving to improve the quality of your work. All work should have joy. The process of continuous improvement can bring that joy to your work. In this chapter, you will begin to establish those conditions that create joy, or the simple satisfaction of knowing that you are doing your work well.

The basic functions of a team are to...

✓ Define your customers and their requirements for the work you deliver to them.
✓ To define your work process that creates the output of products or services that goes to your customer.
✓ To receive feedback on your work and to strive to continuously improve your work process and results.
✓ To provide feedback to your suppliers, who provide the input that you need to do your work in the best possible way.

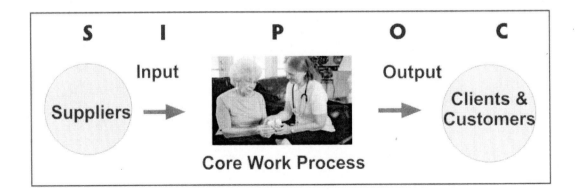

All of these functions can be seen in the above simple diagram and in the acronym SIPOC. In an introductory chapter you defined the components of your SIPOC. Now we are going to be more specific.

The real work of organizations is horizontal, not vertical. We often think of the work we do as being for our manager, in other words, going up the organization. But the real work is not something that is passed up the organization; it is something that flows through the organization, horizontally. A hospital, like most organizations today, is a chain of customer or client relationships.

The above is one way to describe the core work process of a hospital. Each these functions may be a separate department and may be considered one team, or within an area such as clinical care, there are likely numerous teams. But, these teams almost never get their work done alone. They get their work done best by having good customer supplier relationships between each group. Through the eyes of most patients, it is all one big team that is either easy or difficult to navigate.

High performing organizations are passionately focused on managing this flow of work, this core work process that creates the real value of the organization.

WHO ARE OUR CUSTOMERS?

When thinking about your customers, you should consider that some of your customers may be internal in addition to the external customers. Define who some of these internal, as well as customers are.

The Work We Do	The Output of My Work (Knowledge, Service, Materials or Information)	Who Receives this Output? (These are my customers)

Now consider which outputs are most important to your customers.

My Most Important Customer	What is the service or output of my work that is most important to them?	What are the criteria for delighting this customer?
My Next Most Important Customer	What is the service or output of my work that is most important to them?	What are the criteria for delighting this customer?

DEFINING CUSTOMER REQUIREMENTS

Businesses are continually trying to figure out not only what their customers want today, but what they might want tomorrow. Some of the great business success stories, such as Apple Computer, are the result of brilliantly anticipating what will be desired by customers, even before they know anything about it. This sensing of customer needs is a sensibility of any great work or management team.

The following are common categories of criteria for customer satisfaction:

SPECIFICATIONS

What measurements, define the desired service that our customers considers to be a requirement. In a company that makes things, this may include actual dimensions; tolerances between components; weight of the product; surface characteristics such as smoothness or color; or any other measures they may have. What outcome measures are most important to your organization?

RELIABILITY

In a service business, such as healthcare, reliability of service providers may be one of the most important criteria. Do you do what you say you will, and do you perform as the customer expects? Do you show up when you say you will? Do you call back with an answer when you said you would? In other words, not answering the phone is a reliability problem. It says, "I can't rely on this person or team."

TIMELINESS

We have become a "just-in-time" society. We order movies and expect them delivered to our mailbox the next day or instantly over the Internet. We have incredible expectations for things being delivered on time, every time. What are your customer's requirements for timeliness of service delivery?

COURTESY

Even though customers come to you for a specific product or service, they most often judge you by how they feel when they after the service or after they receive the product. Whether or not they feel that they were treated with courtesy and respect has a halo effect on all of their judgments about your service. Included in courtesy is not just "being nice" but listening well, responding to what the customer is saying, and genuinely having empathy, understanding for the customer's needs. Most customers are willing to forgive errors, but have much more trouble forgiving a service provider who refuses to understand the problem they may be causing. We all want to work with other people, either on our team, or with customers and suppliers, who demonstrate compassion and genuine understanding of our needs.

INNOVATION

Another requirement that many customers have, particularly in service companies, is for ways of doing things that are innovative. We like to work with suppliers who are not standing still, but are continually developing better ways to do things, or better products.

Now let's consider how these criteria apply to your customers and the services you provide:

Customer	Product or Service Provided	Requirement
SPECIFICATIONS		
RELIABILITY		
TIMELINESS		
COURTESY		
INNOVATION		

WHAT INPUT DO WE NEED FROM SUPPLIERS?

Just as you are the service provider or supplier to others, there are those who provide you with services, information, materials or knowledge. These "suppliers" may be either internal or they may be external suppliers. Let's identify who are the key suppliers that enable you to do your work in the best possible manner.

My Most Important Input I Need to do my Work	Who Supplies this Input?	What are your key requirements for this Input?

THE POWER OF FEEDBACK

All teams, all people, require feedback for their performance to improve. Feedback is the information we receive that tells us that our performance is increasing, decreasing, or the same. It is a primary source of motivation to change. It is why we step on a scale to weigh ourselves. It is why we attend sports events and continually look up at the scoreboard. It is why we have to keep our eyes on the road when we are driving, so we will know if we are drifting to one side or the other and correct. Feedback keeps us on track. All people need feedback in regard to all performance that matters.

Core work teams or management teams need feedback for all the same reasons that sports teams need feedback. Where does it come from? Basically, there are only three ways we get feedback: first, we generate measures of performance within the team; second we receive feedback from above; and third, we receive feedback from those who receive our work, our customers.

The purpose of this SIPOC model is to establish sources of feedback that will guide our behavior and increase our ability to be self-managing. And, this is the same reason we need to help our suppliers by giving them feedback.

What are the most important types of feedback that you now receive from your customers? Are these subjective ("Nice job") or are they objective measures of performance that can be used as a scorecard?

Feedback Analysis and Improvement			
Who is the Customer?	What Feedback Do We Receive	Is it *Frequent*, *Periodic*, and is it Visually *D*isplayed?	How could this Feedback be Improved?

CHAPTER 10

YOUR TEAM'S SCORECARD & VISUAL DISPLAY

Every high performance team has an effective score keeping system. The purpose of this chapter is to help you establish that system for your team.

OBJECTIVES

1. To have the team reach consensus on their 4 to 8 key measures of performance.

2. To understand the importance of a balanced scorecard.

3. To establish a pattern of data collection and visual display.

Keeping score, taking a count, must be the oldest of all practices of management. Everything that works is not new, and some of the best things are old. Keeping score is as old as the most ancient sport and the most ancient business. Motivation hasn't changed that much in thousands of years. As you implement management you must become very good at "playing the game" that makes work like a sport. The key to that is a good scorekeeping system. It makes work interesting, and it leads to improvement.

Continuous improvement is built on a team structure with accountability for performance. It makes the adult-to-adult assumption that employees and manager are mature, do want to take responsibility for improving performance and, if given the information and skills, will rise to that responsibility. This assumption has rarely proven false.

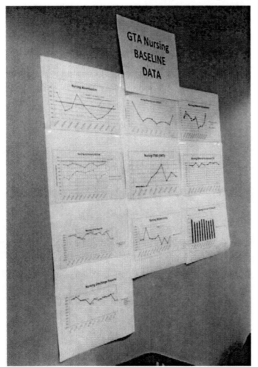

Some years ago my consultants and I were implementing a team process at Eastman Chemicals in Kingsport, Tennessee. I vividly remember a discussion with a department manager when we suggested that financial information on the performance of first level work teams be shared with those teams so they could take responsibility for their business performance. The department manager thought that was ridiculous. He said with great authority "You don't understand these people. These people don't care about that information. They work here just to get their pay check and go home. In fact, you ought to know that most of them consider this their second job."

This was puzzling since this "second job" was eight hours a day at least five days a week. I asked, "So what do they consider their first job, if this is their second job?"

He replied "Well, most of them have their own farms, or some other business that they run. That's what they really care about."

This raised a disturbing question. "What causes these employees to feel more motivation about their own farms or small company then working at Eastman Chemicals?"

That led me to ask this department manager, "Do you think they look at the revenue and cost numbers for their first job?"

"Of course, most of them do their own accounting. They know exactly how well they are doing," he replied.

"Do you think they talk to their customers and are concerned about their satisfaction?" I asked. "Of course, they make darn sure they can sell their produce or product, it's their business."

So these same employees who consider this their "second job" and don't care about the numbers, in their other job they run the business, do the accounting, take responsibility for sales, marketing, quality management, process improvement, and everything else that goes into running a business. This only proves that most often motivation is not simply in the person, but is in the system that surrounds the person.

Hundreds, if not thousands, of times I have seen the person change from someone who "just wants a paycheck" to someone who feels and acts like a business owner and manager because of relatively simple changes in the nature of the system that surrounds them. The essence of that change has always been giving them genuine responsibility for managing a piece of the business, with the information, the authority to make decisions, and the accountability for performance inherent in the assumption of being a "business manager."

SCOREKEEPING IS A SYSTEM OF MOTIVATION

Dr. Deming, the legendary quality leader, used to say that when he visited a manufacturing plant, he wanted to see graphs posted, and he wanted to see dirty fingerprints on the graph. No fingerprints – no good! Why? He wanted to know that those doing the work were literally in touch with the results of their work, their score. Many thought this was a simplistic and foolish idea, but perhaps Dr. Deming understood the same common sense that every team and every coach understands.

The next time you watch a football, baseball, or basketball game have a notepad in your lap and write down every measurement, every kind of score, that is mentioned. In all sports there is a constant reference to numbers. Most of the references are about positive, not negative, numbers – the most balls hit over the fence in right field, the most three pointers shot by a left-handed shooter in the fourth quarter of a game! They seem to have scores on everything. This is what makes it fun to watch and play.

Scorekeeping is also a system that creates unity in groups. Imagine the scoreboard at a basketball or football game – everyone watches it, everyone cheers when it changes, and without it there would be no fans in the stands. What is the magic of the scoreboard? If you understand this, then you understand how to create great scorekeeping systems at work. Something about the way we are internally wired causes us to derive great pleasure in seeing the numbers change; watching the ball go through the hoop, everyone cheers; then their eyes turn to the scoreboard, and they are pleased with the change in score. The entire process helps to bond the team and fans together.

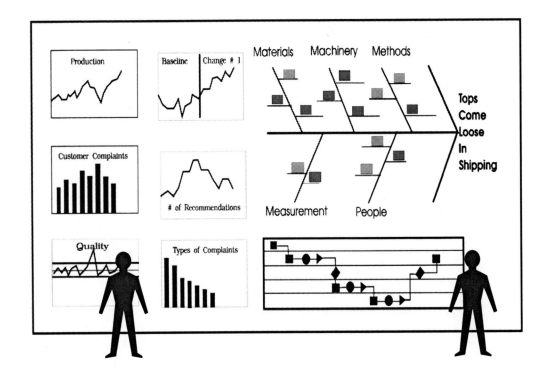

Even those who have no reason to motivate others, but only to motivate themselves, create scorekeeping systems. For example, the lonely runners – those who are able to maintain this behavior for years -- almost all have established a scorekeeping system that keeps them going;

minutes per mile; miles per day, week and month; pulse rate after one or five miles. There are dozens of ways to keep score, and those who maintain their motivation maintain a scorekeeping system. It is the single most obvious essence of self-management. If your team is going to be self-directed it must be self-motivated and this means keeping score.

KEYS TO EFFECTIVE SCOREKEEPING

Here are the keys to scorekeeping that will create the game of continuous improvement:

IMMEDIACY AND FREQUENCY

In basketball, the fans look up at the scoreboard and expect to see a change in one to three seconds after the ball goes through the hoop. In baseball, perhaps because they don't score that often, they have from two to ten seconds. After that amount of time, in either sport, the fans get itchy and may start to show their frustration. If it took an hour to get the score up on the board, how would the fans and players feel? Quickly they would lose motivation and would not show up for the game. How long do your employees or team members wait? The speed and frequency of feedback both increase motivation and increase the effect of a shared experience.

Almost every organization can improve motivation simply by increasing the rate and frequency of feedback. In most organizations, the only reason feedback is delayed is that no one has worked at creating a frequent and immediate feedback system. Investors watch the "real time" ticker and graphs of their investments as they change by the minute or second. With computer technology, creating this kind of feedback is not difficult; we simply need to determine to do it.

VISIBILITY

The United Way gets it. They place a big thermometer graph right at the entrance to the building where you cannot possibly miss it. And every day as you pass it, you don't know why, but you get some little satisfaction in seeing it move up toward its goal. United Way understands the power of good scorekeeping – or good feedback systems.

Providing graphic feedback has advanced in recent years with the addition of computer-based graphics and reporting.

Assess Your Team's Scorekeeping		
Scores for Your Team	Characteristic of Effective Scorekeeping	How Can You Improve Effectiveness?
	Immediacy	
	Frequency	
	Visibility	
	Team Ownership	
	Balanced	

OWNERSHIP

We are excited by a change in numbers when we feel those numbers are for "my team," when we have ownership of that performance, even if it isn't a direct reflection of our own performance. We don't have to be the athlete, but we do have to feel that it is *our team*. And, if we are the athlete, the one performing, you can bet we want measures of our performance, and not someone else's.

It is common for teams to give themselves a name, create their own logo or mascot, and have some piece of clothing made with their team's logo. It is a normal thing to want to identify with a team, root for a team, and follow the scores of a team. There is no reason why all of this cannot be part of your company's work environment. Imagine any environment in which individuals or teams put forth maximum effort, achieve maximum results, and have fun while they are at it. Inevitably, there will be extremely clear scorekeeping, immediate feedback, and visual display of the score.

BALANCED

There was a time when some managers felt that the only thing that mattered was financial results. Those who wanted to elevate the importance of quality measures, customer satisfaction, or process measures had to do battle (and usually lost!) with the financial managers.

Two things have worked to alter the view of most managers today. The first is the surge by Japanese car companies and the adoption of the quest for quality by most major U.S. corporations. These have elevated the understanding of quality and process measures. Almost all managers understand that the way you get to financial measures is through effective processes that are efficient and result in customer satisfaction.

The second is the book by Kaplan & Norton[14] that promoted the idea of a balanced scorecard which proposed a system of balanced measures in the organization.

There is nothing complicated about creating a balanced scorecard. (The trick is more in the process than in the "thing.") Here is a diagram that illustrates the possible components of a balanced scorecard. Kaplan and Norton emphasize that their model and definition of a balanced scorecard is not something fixed in stone, but a proposal that they expect others to modify, adapt, and evolve with their own needs and experience.

When you think about developing your scorecard give consideration to each of the following types of measures:

---

[14] Kaplan, Robert S., Norton, David P. *The Balanced Scorecard: Translating Strategy into Action.* Harvard Business School Press, Boston, 1997.

1. **Customer Satisfaction:** How do you measure customer satisfaction? Do you conduct an annual survey? Do you conduct telephone surveys and ask for feedback in some other way. It is worth considering how we can measure and track improvements in the satisfaction of our customers.

2. **Business Process Measures:** These may be measures of the cycle time from input to output of any process. Or, they may be measures of the number of times rework occurs within the process. Or, any other form of waste or errors that may be caught before the product leaves the organization, but results in unnecessary costs.

3. **Learning and Development**: Every organization must be a learning organization to compete in today's world. Many organizations have goals for how many hours of training are received by each manager or employee. How can you measure the degree of learning and development? Completing the training modules in this workbook could be a measure of learning and development.

4. **Financial Results:** This is obvious at management levels. But, how can we create financial measures at the level of frontline work teams? This is possible. There are costs associated with every work team. The costs of materials, people, space, etc. Those costs can be compared to the percent of revenue attributable to that team. In other words, if a manufacturing plant sold product worth one million dollars a year, and there are one hundred employees in the plant, a team of ten can be considered responsible for that percent of the revenue. Of course, this is not an accurate accounting measure. But, it is a way to give the team a sense of business/financial responsibility for their work.

BUILDING YOUR SCORECARD

Remember that everything that follows is a suggestion as to how to construct your balanced scorecard. Think! You may think of a better way, of variables that are more important, or a better process. But, the following are steps that have proven to work in other organizations and are a pretty good starting point for your own scorecard.

THE PROCESS

The process is as important as the outcome. It is the process of scorekeeping that results in the motivation to continuously improve.

The following five steps to develop each measure should work for you.

1. Define the Score

For each of the four categories brainstorm all the possible measures you can think of. Then ask yourself "Which are the critical few?" There are usually two or three measures in each category that, if improved, will result in corresponding improvement in the other measures. Measuring everything is counterproductive. Measuring the critical few is effective.

When developing your team scorecard, you do not want to have twenty different scores. You want to have four to eight (approximately) scores that are a balanced representation of your team's performance. It is almost always true that, if a team selects twenty different scores, in a short time they will lose track of them and not plot their data on a consistent basis. Keep it simple.

2. Baseline Data

How do you know when you have improved? Before you change anything to seek improvement, it is very helpful to have baseline data that will give you a basis to determine whether or not you are making changes that are effective.

Below you will see a graph with baseline data recorded and then the data after the team has made a change in their work process. You can see that the baseline performance is stable. This is important because if there is already an upward trend in performance, how will you know that a new change is making a difference? It is better to let that trend play out; let it get to the point of achieving stability. Then you can implement a change to your process and you will be able to see the difference.

Most importantly, notice how easy it is to see the point of improvement on the graph. Clearly whatever the team did made a positive difference. By seeing the change occur on the graph after they have made a change, the team is learning. They are learning by using the scientific method, which is simply to know the facts of performance by collecting data, then making a change that might affect performance, and then observing the "post-intervention" data.

You can also see that there is a goal line on the graph. When a team sets a goal that they put on the graph, it gives them something to shoot for, something to celebrate when they succeed. Again, seeing it on the graph is extremely helpful to motivate the team.

3. Set Objectives and Visualize

We are not talking about "management-by-objectives". We are talking about YOUR team setting objectives for YOUR own performance. It is the difference between being "managed" and "self-managing." Look at the graph of your performance. Then look at what improvements you think you need to make based on the feedback you received from your customers. In later chapters, we will discuss problem-solving methods that will help you make these improvements.

4. Change

In later chapters you will look more thoroughly at specific problems you will find in your process and institute changes. Your period of implementing changes may be days or months. The important thing is that you are going to plot your data and keep track of the effect of your changes as a team.

5. Evaluate

The focus of your team meetings should be on this scorecard and what you are doing to improve it. You should be discussing whether or not your changes are having the desired effect and whether or not the data is stable or trending in one direction or another.

BRAINSTORM AND DECIDE ON SCORECARD MEASURES

You scorecard should be a living thing. In other words, as you learn and develop the skills of team management you will modify and improve your scorecard.

Now it is time for your team to consult together, brainstorm together, and reach consensus together on the scores that would be most indicative of your team's performance.

Remember that you do not want more than six to eight scores that you monitor as a team. Also, please remember to make the score visible. Graph it!!! Post it on the wall where your team meets or works. Remember the scoreboard at the basketball game. Don't cover it up!

BUILD YOUR BALANCED SCORECARD

CATEGORY	MEASURES	WHERE WILL DATA COME FROM?	WHERE WILL IT BE DISPLAYED?
Customer Satisfaction Measures			
Process Measures			
Learning and Development Measures			
Financial or Productivity Measures			

PART TWO
IMPROVING PERFORMANCE

CHAPTER 11

SOLVING PROBLEMS

The purpose of this chapter is to provide your team with a simple and effective model of problem-solving. Solving problems is one of the most important functions of every team.

OBJECTIVES

1. To understand a healthy philosophy of problem-solving.

2. To introduce and practice a simple and quick method of problem-solving (PDCA).

3. To introduce and practice a more comprehensive model of problem-solving for more complex problems (A3).

At the heart of the work of every team is solving problems and making improvements in their process and performance. Before exploring methods of problem-solving, it is important to think about the philosophy of problem-solving.

Many organizations are crippled by the wrong philosophy, and no methods will overcome the wrong philosophy. We must have a healthy philosophy of problem-solving.

A Philosophy of Problem-solving

Problems are Normal!

You should solve problems every day. Your managers should solve problems every day. Solving problems is our job. It is why we come to work. If we had no problems, we would be terrifically bored. Celebrate problems! Every problem is an opportunity for learning.

Unfortunately, in the "old culture" before teams and lean, it was common for managers to punish those who presented problems. They thought you were doing your job if you had no problems and brought no problems to them.

Dr. Deming said that to improve we should "drive out fear." He was addressing this philosophy of problem-solving. Fear hides problems, but it does not solve them.

The Problem is in the Process, Not in the Person

Most problems can be solved by examining how we do things, the work process. Just as health problems are often caused by the routine ways we live, most problems at work are the result of the routine, habitual, ways we get things done. Of course, sometimes they are the result of individuals not being adequately trained or informed. But, this lack of training or lack of information is, itself, a process problem. If you blame individuals for problems, you will again create fear and cause them to hide those problems. It is far better to say "I am sure you wanted to get a better result; let's see what caused the problem." By analyzing the problem, rather than blaming the person, you will find it much easier to make progress.

Fast is Good and Quicker is Better

Every problem has a cost that occurs in time. Health problems are exactly the same. The longer you ignore or delay solving a health problem, the more likely it is to get worse and be more difficult to solve. If a problem is causing anxiety for a customer, with every passing day the probability increases that the customer will find another supplier. These costs are usually invisible because customers rarely tell you why they chose to buy a competitor's product or service. They generally do not consider that their responsibility. So it is your responsibility to find problems and solve them quickly.

THERE ARE NO PERFECT SOLUTIONS

Every day of our life is an experiment. We experiment with new items on the menu of a restaurant. We experiment with a new variety of soup when we go to the supermarket. We experiment with a new traffic route, a new television program, or a new website. We are constantly experimenting. This is how we learn.

In our daily life we recognize that we will never find the one right and final website, or the final menu item or food in the grocery store. Why do we think we will find the perfect and final solution to any problem at work?

When we are solving problems, we are only finding the best solution we can find NOW with the facts and information we currently have. A week or month from now we will have new facts or information that may make a different solution seem better. Accepting this reality makes it that much easier to get on with the experimentation of implementing solutions. Every solution is a learning opportunity.

ADDRESS PROBLEMS THAT YOUR TEAM CAN CONTROL

It is always more fun to find problems that someone else should fix. It is why we enjoy sports or politics. We think politicians should fix everything, and we enjoy pointing out what a terrible job they are doing. This is fun because we are spectators. We don't have to change our self.

Your team should address problems that are within your control.

TRUST IN THE POWER OF COLLECTIVE INTELLIGENCE

Let us assume that you are the smartest person on your team. But the reality is that our knowledge and intelligence is only a fraction of the combined knowledge and intelligence of the combined team. Just imagine if you could somehow lift out of each brain their experience, wisdom, and intelligence and put it in a pile in the middle of a table. Now put your brainpower on the table next to it. Your brainpower will be small in comparison.

The magic of effective group problem-solving is that the collective brain power of the group expands to the degree that it combines. In other words, if you and I have an open conversation about a problem, it is likely that there will emerge a solution which will be something that neither of us would have arrived at on our own. There is no way that your individual brainpower can match the collective intelligence of the group... if the group is able to create collective intelligence.

I WANT THE FACTS, NOTHING BUT THE FACTS!

Many years ago, before most readers of this workbook were born, there was a television detective show, probably the first "cops and robbers," show called *Dragnet*. Sergeant Friday was the central character. In each show he would interview some witness to a crime, and he would always say "I just want the facts, nothing but the facts."

It is easy to form opinions. The moment someone walks into the room, we form an opinion of them. But we don't know them. We don't know the facts. We don't know what happened at home this morning; we don't know what pain they are suffering; we don't know what they can contribute. Opinions without facts are easy. But effective problem-solving is always based on a period of gathering the facts. Too often we think we know the facts when we only know some small portion of the facts.

Think about how problems are solved in your team. How is the above philosophy of problem-solving practiced, or not? What would you do differently if you adopted this philosophy?

THE PDCA PROBLEM-SOLVING MODEL (A4)

For many years, even before the quality movement or lean management, there were many models of problem-solving. Many writers have defined the five, six, or seven steps to problem-solving. Most of these models include the same or very similar elements. There is no one right model or one best way. All problem-solving processes should include fact finding, brainstorming and investigating the causes of a problem, brainstorming and deciding on solutions, and action planning and follow-up. These are the most critical common elements in all problem-solving models.

When the Total Quality Management process was the primary model improvement model the PDCA (Plan, Do, Check and Act) cycle of problem-solving was very popular. It is also known as the Schewhart Cycle after Walter Schewhart a pioneer in the quality field. However, it was made popular by another quality guru, Dr. Edwards Deming. It was adopted as a common problem-solving model at many companies.

The PDCA cycle is best used for relatively simple problems, although you can place many different methods or steps within these four major steps.

On the next two pages you will see a blank PDCA form you can use, and a form with more detailed steps within each of the four major steps.

- **Plan** to improve your operations first by finding out what things are going wrong (that is identify the problems), and come up with ideas for solving these problems.

- **Do** changes designed to solve the problems on a small or experimental scale first. This minimises disruption to routine activity while testing whether the changes will work or not.

- **Check** whether the small scale or experimental changes are achieving the desired result or not. Also, continuously Check key activities (regardless of any experimentation going on) to ensure that you know what the quality of the output is at all times to identify any new problems when they crop up.

- **Act** to standardize procedures or process and implement changes on a larger scale if the experiment is successful. This means making the changes a routine part of your activity. Also Act to involve other persons (other departments, suppliers, or customers) affected by the changes and whose cooperation you need to implement them on larger scale, or those who may simply benefit from what you have learned (you may, of course, already have involved these people in the "Do" or trial stage)

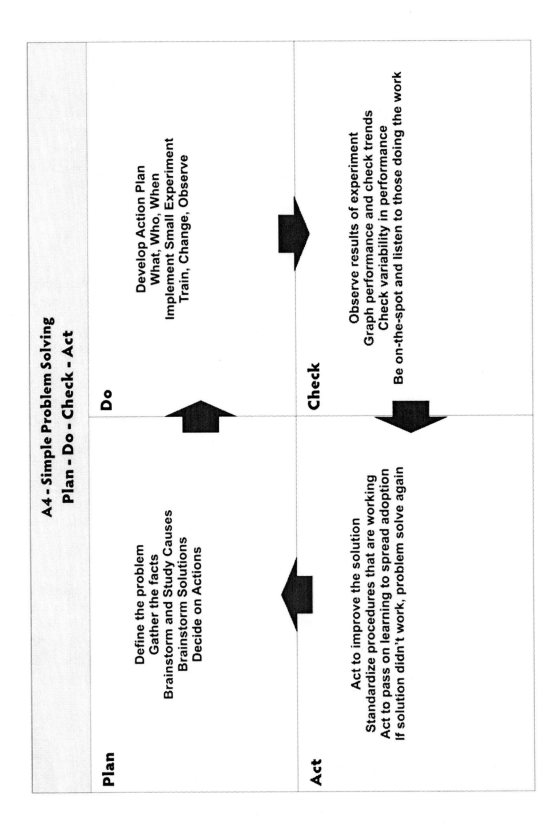

A4 - Simple Problem Solving
Plan - Do - Check - Act

Plan

Define the problem
Gather the facts
Brainstorm and Study Causes
Brainstorm Solutions
Decide on Actions

Do

Develop Action Plan
What, Who, When
Implement Small Experiment
Train, Change, Observe

Check

Observe results of experiment
Graph performance and check trends
Check variability in performance
Be on-the-spot and listen to those doing the work

Act

Act to improve the solution
Standardize procedures that are working
Act to pass on learning to spread adoption
If solution didn't work, problem solve again

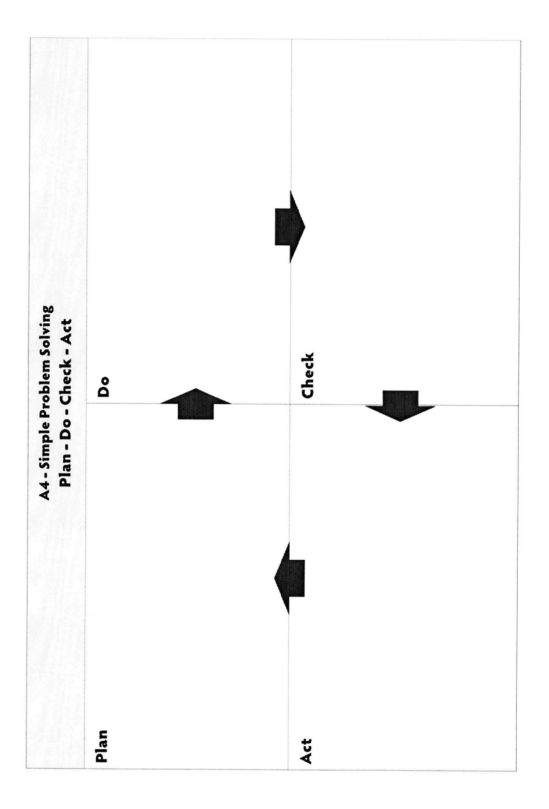

A4 - Simple Problem Solving
Plan - Do - Check - Act

Plan

Do

Check

Act

THE A3 PROBLEM-SOLVING MODEL

The following is a more comprehensive and explicit problem-solving model. It contains all the same elements as the PDCA and a few more. This is recommended for problems that require more in-depth problem-solving.

The PDCA model is simple enough to use on one sheet of paper, and A3 sheet that is about the size of these pages. The following model can also be used on one page, but it fits much better on a larger sheet, an A3. These A3 and A4 forms will be available from your coaches.

This model can be summarized by the acronym DIMPABAC: *Define* the problem to be solved; *Inquire* with all those who have facts regarding the problem to gain different understanding and insight; *Measure* actual performance on the problem; *Principles* should be defined that are important to understanding this problem and its solution; *Analyze* the data and causes of the problem; *Brainstorm* solutions to the problem; Agree to *Act* on a solution; *Control* and standardize the process and evaluate results.

1. DEFINE THE PROBLEM

D
I
M
P
A
B
A
C

Define
↓
Inquire
↓
Measure
↓
Principles
↓
Analyze
↓
Brainstorm
↓
Act
↓
Control

What makes for a good problem definition? Imagine that you are not feeling well and you go to your doctor's office. Now let's imagine that there are three doctors there. Immediately after you walk into the office the three doctors stare at you at the same time. One doctor looks at you and says "Darn, she really looks sick." The second doctor looks at you and says "I don't see it. She looks fine to me." And, the third doctor says, "Well exactly where does it hurt and how long has it felt that way? Let's take some tests and measure a few of your vital signs and then let's make a judgment."

In which of these doctors do you have the most confidence? I think it would be the third one. Why? Because, the first two doctors are telling you how they feel, rather than how you feel, based on little information. Their judgments have as much to do with them as they do with you. The judgment that you look "really sick" is pretty useless. It is a very inadequate problem definition. Every doctor knows that you cannot begin to prescribe a remedy until you have a good definition of the problem – where it hurts, how long it has hurt, exactly where the pain is, etc. Similarly, your problem definition should be specific and it should be based on hard data.

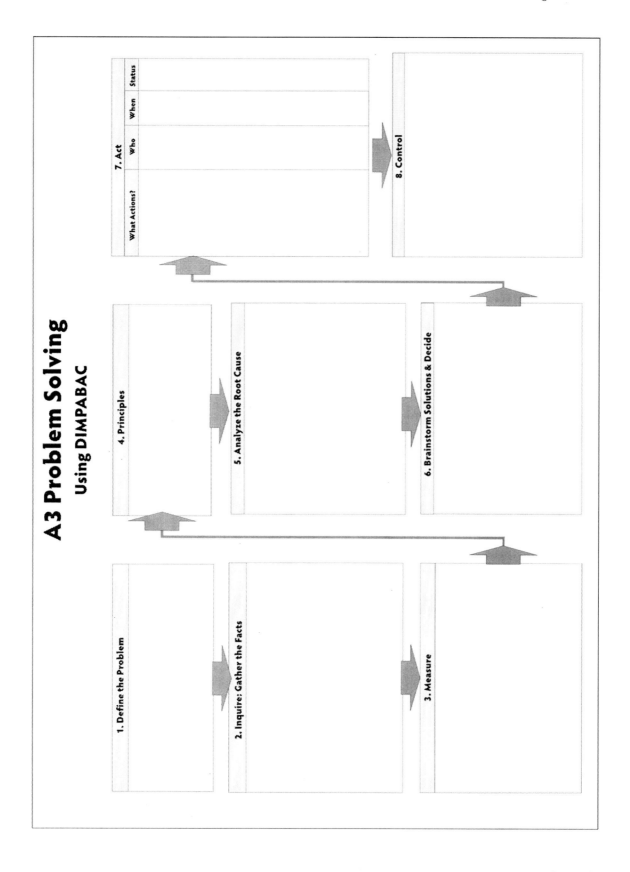

A3 Problem Solving
Using DIMPABAC

7. Act

What Actions?	Who	When	Status

8. Control

4. Principles

5. Analyze the Root Cause

6. Brainstorm Solutions & Decide

1. Define the Problem

2. Inquire: Gather the Facts

3. Measure

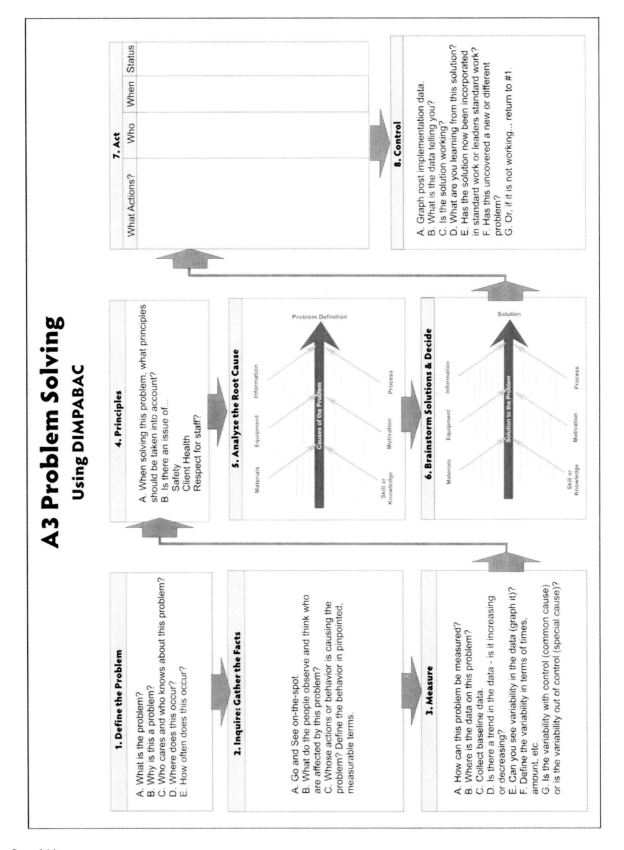

A good problem definition has what is called "inter-observer reliability." This is a fancy way of saying that if three or four people see the same thing, they will be able to reach the same conclusion. The description will allow all of them to know it when they see it. For example, if you are describing a problem of a hitter in baseball, you might say that he is a "weak hitter." This may be true, but there is not likely to be inter-observer reliability. Two observers could easily get into an argument as to whether this player is a "weak" hitter. On the other hand, if you say that this hitter has an on-base percentage of .165, assuming your facts are correct, this is hard to argue with. Two people looking at the facts would agree on this definition of the problem. The problem to be solved is "how to increase his on-base percentage." That definition is a measure of performance.

You could also describe the problem in terms of *pinpointed behavior*. You could describe how this player is slow to get the bat off his shoulder and is late to swing 50% of the time. Two observers, if they were trained and observed carefully, would likely come up with the same definition of the problem or be able to recognize the problem you have described.

These more specific definitions are far more helpful in leading us to a solution than simply to say that this ball player is a "weak" hitter.

Pick a problem that is important to your team. This problem should be one that will improve some measure on your scorecard. You have already interviewed customers, you have developed a scorecard, and you have mapped your process. You should be prepared to solve some important problem facing your team. Answer the following questions:

What is the problem definition?

_____

_____

How long has this been a problem?

_____

How does this problem affect performance or business results?

_____

_____

How can you measure this problem in terms of performance or behavior?

_____

_____

2. INQUIRE: GATHER THE FACTS

Sometimes when you begin to solve a problem, you will have all the experts and information in the room. However, it is very common that this is not the case. For most problems, you will have to do a bit more homework to gain input from others. It is almost always true that the team that is in control of the problem (in other words they may be the cause) do not have the same understanding as customer, suppliers, or other experts.

Go and see where the problem is. There is no substitute for being on-the-spot and directly observing the problem. In lean management there is a popular term – *Gemba*, or the *Gemba Walk*. It simply means going to where the work is being done. Too often managers make judgments without being on-the-spot.

Who has expertise in this problem - customer, supplier, other teams, internal experts?

_____

_____

_____

What information would you like to know about this problem from others?

_____

_____

_____

_____

Who will interview these persons and when?

_____

_____

Have we learned anything that may redefine the problem?

_____

_____

What have we learned that may suggest a solution?

_____

_____

3. Measure the Problem

You don't know how serious a problem is until you measure and build a baseline set of data. You will remember in a previous chapter on scorekeeping we discussed the importance of establishing a baseline so that you would then know whether or not you are improving. This will also tell you the severity of the problem.

By looking at a graph of your data you can tell many things that can guide your decisions to make improvement. For example, you may see the variations in performance, and this may point to causes of the problem. You may also see trends. In the following graph you will see three different lines. One of them demonstrates relatively stable performance. Performance is not the same every day; it varies, but it varies in a way that tells you that it is not getting better or getting worse. The other two trend lines show increasing performance or declining performance. It is extremely important that you observe the slope of the trend line before trying to make changes.

If your performance is in an improving trend, should you make a change at all? Perhaps it would be better to let the data continue to improve under the current conditions. Eventually it will come to a level at which it will stabilize or start to decline. If you implement an improvement, while the trend line is already improving, you will have no way to know whether or not your change has had any affect. On the other hand you may wish to make some change quickly to stop a declining trend. However, you should analyze the causes of this decline to understand what conditions are driving down performance.

4. Principles: What is Important?

As your team is about to solve a problem, it will be helpful if you ask the team, "What is important to make a solution a successful solution? What really matters?"

For example, you may recognize that a solution will require cooperation from other teams or from managers or staff. Therefore, you may decide that a principle for an effective solution is *"We will invite those interested managers and staff to contribute to our analysis and solution."* Or, your organization may have strategic goal, for example to reduce costs, and you may decide that a principle is *"The solution must contribute to cost reduction."*

Principles are based on an understanding of the context, what is happening in your organization or sometimes the political reality of the organization. These things, in addition to the needs of your customers, define what is important.

When looking for problem-solving principles, you should go back to the team's principles and purpose you established in one of the first steps in the team process. How do those values affect the problem you are trying to solve or the solution you are looking for? What other principles should guide your search for a solution?

BRAINSTORMING – GETTING CREATIVE

Brainstorming has been used for many years since WWII when it was developed to stimulate innovation and creativity in research laboratories. The idea is simple. It is our normal habit, when working in groups, to jump to a solution and to immediately start criticizing or judging a solution or ideas offered by someone else. The big breakthrough in brainstorming is the research-proven idea that we will generate more ideas, and more creative ideas, if we suspend judgment or criticism and focus on generating a lot of ideas. One idea stimulates a second idea, which in turn stimulates a third. There is what feels like a chemical reaction between the minds of the team members when they allow themselves the freedom of brainstorming.

Brainstorming requires disciplined leadership. In other words, the facilitator of the brainstorming must be prepared to stop someone who starts to judge the ideas of someone else. This will put the brake on idea generation. Here are some steps to effective brainstorming:

- ☑ Clearly define the problem that is the subject of brainstorming. Ask the group whether they understand the boundaries of the problem.
- ☑ Make it visual. Seeing ideas is essential to stimulating ideas in other team members. Write them on a flip chart, a cause-and-effect diagram, or an affinity diagram (see the next few pages for a description of affinity diagrams).
- ☑ Don't rush. Give it time. It takes time to think.
- ☑ Give everyone an opportunity to contribute. You can go "round-robin" around the room in sequence, use slips of paper, or just

"free-wheel" letting anyone speak when they want to. It is often effective to switch between these methods in the same session.

☑ Ask clarifying questions when you don't understand someone's idea. "In other words are you saying that ... may be the cause?" And allow the team member to respond with a clarifying statement.

☑ The group should feel free to combine ideas or build one idea on top of another.

☑ Encourage wild and crazy ideas. Someone might say "I think we should just tear the place down and start over." Rather than saying "Well, you know we can't do that," allow it. Then someone might think, "Well if we did have the freedom to start over, what would we do differently?" And that thought may lead to another, etc. Crazy ideas often generate the most useful ideas.

☑ Humor is often the sign of creative thinking. Laughter is good.

5. ANALYZE (BRAINSTORM) THE ROOT CAUSE

At this stage you will want to have your team brainstorm all of the possible causes of the problem. Probably the most effective tool for brainstorming causes and solutions is the "fishbone" or "cause-and-effect" diagram. On the following diagram you can see five major categories of potential causes. The original categories were Man, Machine, Materials and Methods. These are not necessarily the most appropriate ones for your team and for this problem. Your team should discuss and reach consensus on the four to six most likely big potential categories of causes. Then, under each of these brainstorm the possible causes.

GENERATING IDEAS

There are several ways to do this. One way is for the facilitator to simply write down the causes as members of the team think of them. Another way is for everyone to write down possible causes individually on Post-it-Notes, then come up to the wall and place those notes on the fishbone diagram where they belong. It is a good idea to do this silently so members of the team take time to think. As a member of the team sees another member place a note by "Incorrect Information", for example, that may stimulate an idea in his or her head. That may lead to thinking of a different possible cause.

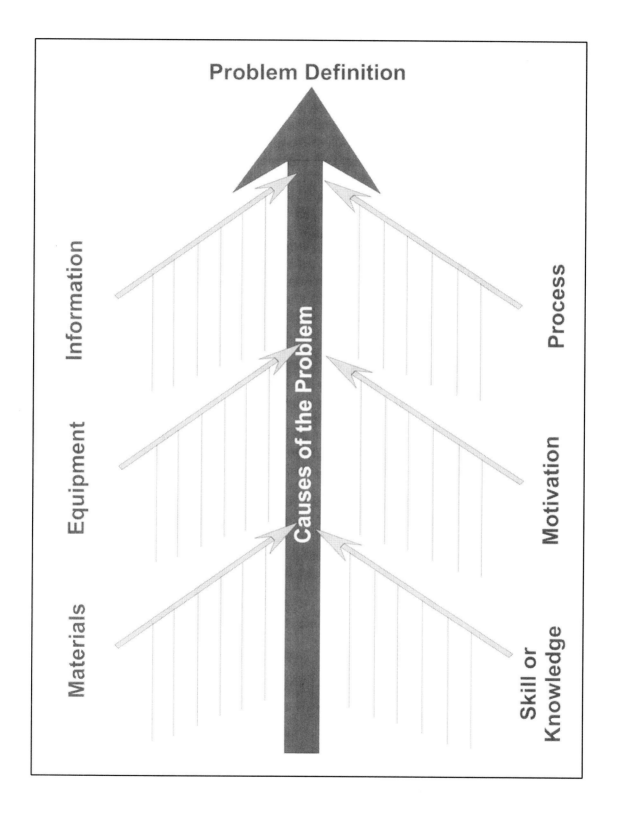

It is usually assumed that this brainstorming will occur in one meeting. However, this may not be the best way to discover causes or solutions to problems. CEDAC is "cause-and-effect-diagrams with the addition of cards". The idea is to put a large fishbone diagram on the wall where everyone can see it. Sometimes it may be in the hall where associates arrive or leave work. On this diagram place the definition of a major problem. In an envelope by the diagram, place a set of large 3"X5" notes. Have notes of two different colors. Indicate a code that blue, for example, are the "cause" cards; while yellow may be "solution" cards. Team members can then think about the problem and place cards there whenever they like.

Another way to brainstorm is to use an "affinity diagram." This is also a very simple idea. Again, use Post-it-Notes. Members of the team write down what they think are the likely causes of the problem. Each cause is written on a separate note. The team members then just go up to a bare wall and post the notes on the wall in a random manner.

After members have been given some time, perhaps fifteen minutes, to do this, the facilitator then asks them to silently sort them into "like" causes. These like causes may be categories like those on the fishbone diagram. They are organizing the causes into "affinity" groups.

It is contrary to the group's habits to work in silence. But there is a magic to silence. People have to think! Very often we talk first and think later. Now we are being asked to think first, and we will talk later.

The members of the team will move the notes into clusters that they think go together. If one member thinks a note belongs in a different cluster, it can be moved there. If someone else moves it back, then the team may recognize that it can logically belong in more than one cluster, and a duplicate can be made.

"Affinity Diagram"
Causes of Late Delivery

Once the group is finished, it is time for a discussion of the different clusters.

Why are they clustered together?

What is the common idea or principle that holds a cluster together?

Are the notes truly separate causes or do some of them overlap or duplicate each other?

What are we learning from this?

Are some clusters more important than others? Or are some of them related to each other.

REACHING CONSENSUS ON PRIORITIES

Now that you have generated many possible causes of a problem, it is time to narrow them down to a critical few. You may also wish to study them further. But, first narrow them so you can focus your energy on solving the most important causes of a problem.

Here is a simple way to reach consensus on priorities.

- Narrow the List

    Let us assume that you have a flip chart with a list of twenty-five possible causes of the problem you are trying to solve. Ask the team members to look at this list and pick the five that they think are the most significant causes of the problem. The facilitator can ask the members of the group to come to the flip chart, take a magic marker, and make a small dot by each of the five they have selected. When they have all voted, it will be easy to see which five received the most votes.

    At this point it is a good idea to ask the group "Do you all agree that these five are the five most significant priorities for us to work on? Does anyone want to make a case for something else?" Generally, the group will agree, but sometimes someone will feel strongly about another one, and it may be that others do not understand the issue in the same way that he or she does. You can ask the group if they agree to add this as a sixth item.

    Now you can decide whether five are too many to pursue further. You may want to get the list down to the two causes to really focus your energies. If this is the case, you can now ask the group to vote again. But, before voting a second time, it is a good idea to ask someone to argue the case for each of the causes remaining on the list. This is often a healthy discussion in which one or two members may be able to provide information that only they have.

- Reach Consensus

    Either by voting again, or by a simple show of hands, you may now reach consensus. When reaching consensus, it is important for the leader or facilitator to state the decision being made and ask everyone if they agree. The facilitator should simply look at the group and see if all are nodding their heads. If not, the facilitator should seek clarification.

PARETO ANALYSIS

The other, and more scientific way to prioritize, is to do a Pareto Analysis. The above process of prioritizing may be based entirely on how the members of the team "feel" about different causes of the problem. Sometimes those feelings are well grounded, and sometimes they are not.

To do a Pareto Analysis you must have data on the different causes of the problem. Once you have narrowed the potential causes down to five or ten, you may decide to go collect data to determine exactly how often the problem is caused by each.

Let's use the example of a team of employees who work in a movie theater. They have a form at the exit from the theater on which customers are encouraged to give feedback. You have taken the cards for a one month period and sorted all of the complaints. Here is the list of complaints and the number of each. You will also see the percent this represents of the total.

1. Dirty floors in theater – 97 (45.3%)
2. Dirty rest rooms – 65 (30.3%)
3. Movie started late – 27 (21.6?)
4. Bad popcorn – 13 (06%)
5. Discourteous employees – 7 (.03%)
6. Temperature in theater – 5 (.02%)

Total = 214 complaints

214 complaints equal 100% of the total complaints. Below you can see a bar graph representing the number of complaints by category and a

line representing the total percent represented by each column, cumulatively, so it ends at 100%.

Looking at this chart, you can see that the first two "critical few" causes represent 75% of the total complaints. If you could eliminate those two problems you would have eliminated 75% of the causes of dissatisfaction on the part of customers. It may be possible to focus on all of the problems. However, on many teams it is not possible to focus on everything at once; rather it is most effective to pick one or two on which to focus your energies. Pareto analysis has proven an effective way of prioritizing problem-solving efforts.

6. BRAINSTORM SOLUTIONS

You have now gathered a great deal of information on your problem. You have thought about it a great deal. Now it is time to think about and define those solutions.

Start by brainstorming solutions. Use the same brainstorming techniques, including the fishbone diagram, affinity diagram and other techniques but this time in a search for solutions to the specific causes you have defined.

It is wise to NOT feel that you have to decide on a solution in one meeting. Often you need to study solutions. You may need to consult with an engineer if the solution involves changes in equipment. You may need to consult with human resource professionals regarding the need for additional training if that is part of your solution.

When you consider possible solutions, consider experimenting. Do not assume that you have to "bet" that you have made the one right decision. It is dangerous to tie your ego to a solution. Even with the best problem-solving methods, we are often wrong. It is okay to be wrong if you are willing to take action, evaluate, learn, and modify your solution. Thomas Edison tried thousands of "solutions" before inventing the light bulb. There is no reason to think that you will discover the one "right" solution on your first try. If you become too invested in one solution, it may make you blind to other opportunities or other solutions.

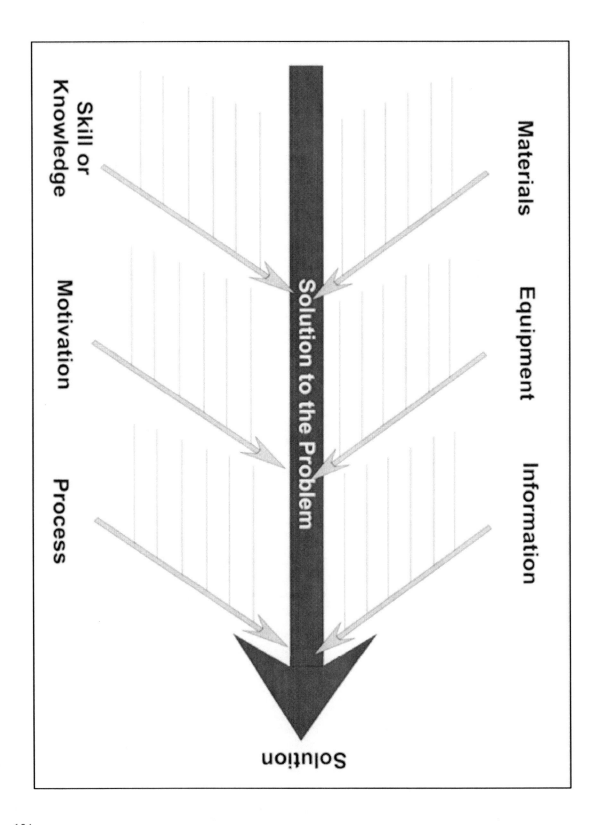

7. Action Planning – Take Action

Now you have to be a manager. You have to manage the implementation of solutions. This is not difficult, but it requires a disciplined approach. On the following page you will find an Action Planning Worksheet that will be helpful.

Every action plan should include the following simple elements:

What Action Needs to be Taken: Make a list of the specific actions that need to be taken to implement your chosen solution. Be as specific as possible when listing these action steps. List them in the order you think they need to occur.

Who will take the action: It is very helpful to put this simple action planning sheet on a flip chart at the front of the room as you develop the action plan. As you write down each action step that is agreed to by the team, ask "Who will do this?" It isn't going to happen if no one commits to taking responsibility for action. Write down the name or initials of the person who commits to act.

When will the action be completed? The person who agreed to take the action should now commit to a completion date.

Status: Following the development of this action plan, it should be reviewed at each meeting of the team. If you have the action plan on a flip chart page, it is a good idea to bring that and put it on the wall. The knowledge that this will be on the wall and that it will be reviewed is the best form of accountability. When we know that we are going to be held accountable for our commitments, we think seriously about them and hold ourselves accountable for getting the action completed.

8. Control for Results and Review

Control simply means to continue measuring your process and results. This is why you have a scorecard. You should now see changes on your graphs. If not, then why not?

Solving problems almost always requires repeated analysis and brainstorming solutions. You should never feel like a failure when you do not get the results you hoped for. Be a scientist. Learn from your results, experiment again, watch the results again, and you will discover the best solution.

Action Plan			
Problem:			
Solution:			
Action-What?	**Who Will Act?**	**When?**	**Status**

Chapter 12

Motivation and Human Performance

The purpose of this chapter is to help the team members manage their own motivation.

Objectives

1. To learn a model of analyzing and solving human performance problems.

2. To help the team their own motivation and the motivation of others.

3. To learn to use positive reinforcement effectively – to practice 4 to1.

A high performing culture is one of shared appreciation, a culture in which we love coming to work both because of the intrinsic satisfaction of serving our customers, but also because of the support and appreciation we receive from our colleagues.

Human motivation is a subject on which there have been more theories developed and more books written than almost any other. Debates about the source of motivation go back to the Greek philosophers, Plato and Aristotle. Much of the debate about motivation has been about whether motivation comes from within the individual or is the result of outside forces in the environment. Entire schools of psychology have grown up around these two ideas.

It is safe to say that human motivation is complicated and there are a lot of individual and cultural differences in how we are motivated. But there are also some universal motivations although they may appear different in different cultures. One way to understand motivation is to consider that there are three levels of motivation: the *spiritual*, the *social* and the *situational*.

MOTIVATIONS OF THE HUMAN SPIRIT: THE PURPOSE PRINCIPLE

The spiritual level of motivation refers to those things that are very deep personal beliefs and values. Your religious faith, your family, and

your country may all be sources of motivation at this spiritual level. Motives at this level are almost always focused on the very long term. You will sacrifice for achieving a goal in the afterlife. You will sacrifice much of your own pleasure for the well-being of your family. And many have willingly sacrificed their own lives for their country and their faith.

While no one at work will ask you to sacrifice your life, there are still spiritual motivations in the world of work. Knowing that your organization has a worthy purpose, is doing something worthy for society, and is creating a positive legacy, is a key to motivation. It is not something that you will see reported in this month's scorecard, but it is something that will cause people to make sacrifices for the organization. We all want to know that we work for a worthy organization that does important work.

Purpose is the most pure energy source emerging from the deepest well of our soul. It is the answer to every important question about our being. Why are we here? Where are we going? What difference will it make if we get there? It is the motivation of motivations, it is not merely what people will work for, it is what people will die for. The pursuit of purpose was in the beginning and it was "the Word." Without it you are nothing, mere dust, because you are going nowhere and don't know why.

Purpose is found at many levels – common and profound. Earning money to feed and educate your children is a sensible purpose. Sacrificing for a church or charity, enlisting in public service and even politics, may be motivated by a genuine desire to contribute to the betterment of fellow citizens. Of course, not every purpose is noble and inspiring. The cocaine dealer, the politician appealing to fears and hatreds, the business person seeking personal gain without regard to the interests of others, are all fulfilling a perverse purpose. But, there are natural laws. We are all tempted to pick the apple off the tree rather than defer gratification. Even though we have knowledge of our best long-term interests, we would rather just grab the ice cream than resist our temptation and do what we know to be in our long-term self-interest.

Something within our nature, perhaps it is a seed planted by God within us, determines that we all seek and will sacrifice for that which is noble. Every leader understands, perhaps intuitively, that followers will sacrifice for a noble purpose, and the leader defines the mission of the organization in terms of a worthy purpose. We will sacrifice, even our lives, for a cause, we perceive to be noble and worthy. Why? Because we understand the mystery of sacrifice and when we sacrifice our money, time, or energy to that which we hold to be noble, there is no sacrifice, but only an investment – one with a guaranteed return – and that return is in that which is most precious to us, our own nobility and worth. The mystery of sacrifice is that we become like that unto which we sacrifice ourselves. When we sacrifice our self to that which is noble, we become more noble.

Just ask yourself how you felt the last time you sacrificed your time, money or energy to something you believed to be noble (your faith, family, country or community). How did you feel? You felt better about yourself. You felt more worthy. You felt more worthy because you became like that unto which you sacrificed. Conversely, the person who sits home all day glued to the boob tube, sacrificing himself to the trivial, becomes himself, more trivial. And how does he feel about himself? He feels depressed and less worthy. And he or she is witnessing the same truth that he is becoming like that unto he sacrifices himself.

In Jack London's novel *Martin Eden* there is a wonderful line – *"God's own mad lover should die for the kiss, but not for thirty thousand dollars a year."* God's own mad lover, the seeker after that which is noble, will die for the kiss, to be near, to touch, that which is most noble; but, not for the material and transitory thing. This is the mystery of sacrifice. This is the mystery by which human energy is created.

Leaders lead by communicating a sense of purpose. Followers respond with pleasure because they know that by sacrificing their energies they will be ennobled in return. This is the contract between the leader and the led and when it is fulfilled they become a unified whole.

What are your sources of spiritual motivation, higher purpose, and how does that affect your motivation at work?

SOCIAL MOTIVATIONS

One of the intentions of the team process is to increase the motivation that comes from working with a group, your team members. Social motivations are those that define who you are in relation to other people. It is innate in the human species to seek friendship, family, association, and a respected status among those whom we value. There are not many among us who would want to go live on a mountain top by ourselves as a hermit. It may seem like an interesting escape for a short time, but most of us could not stand the loneliness and isolation for long.

Just as the family farm and craft shop were a strong source of social support one hundred years ago, the work or management team, as well as the larger social network in our organization, can serve as a system of needed social support. A healthy social system tends to make individuals psychologically healthy. A dysfunctional social system creates personal dysfunction. This rule can easily be seen in the social system of the family. We all know of examples of dysfunctional families producing dysfunctional individuals.

Take some time to think about healthy families and their parallel in the work place.

Why do healthy families tend to produce healthy individuals? What are the important elements of this social system?

_____

_____

How do these characteristics relate to teams in your area? Is there anything that your team could do to strengthen the social support system at work?

_____

_____

_____

SITUATIONAL MOTIVATION

Situational motivations are those that occur from our environment. Management systems tend to focus on these sources of motivation because they are most easy to modify.

Behavioral psychology, or behavior analysis, is the study of how the environment affects human behavior. There is a great deal of research that clearly demonstrates that you can increase (or decrease) performance by controlling those events that come before and after behavior. This is not a new revelation, nor is it complicated.

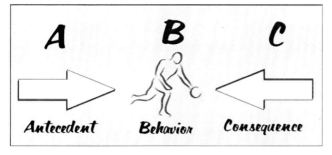

One simple way of remembering this model is to think about the "A-B-C" Model. The "A" is for antecedents. An antecedent is something that comes before and acts as a *prompt* or *cue* for behavior. It triggers the behavior. Red light, green light, stop signs and a thousand other things that we see every day are antecedents for some specific behavior.

The "B" is for the desired behavior, such as taking your foot off the gas and putting it on the brake at a stop sign. The "C" is for consequences. When you stop for a stop light, the consequence is not having an accident. If you don't stop there is a good chance of an accident or a traffic ticket. It is clear that the antecedent and the consequences in this case serve as motivation for the behavior of stopping your car at the stop light.

ANTECEDENTS: STIMULUS CONTROL

Antecedents and consequences, to use the technical term, are both stimuli. But, every stimulus doesn't have control over every behavior. Only some stimuli have control, or influence, over some behavior. Why? What makes some behavior come under the influence of some stimulus?

We *learn* to respond to an antecedent. What does this mean? The traffic sign on the freeway says 65MPH. How fast is the traffic going? Probably 75 MPH. Why? Because you know that if you are going 75MPH there is no consequence. Actually, there is a positive consequence for going faster than 65MPH. It is pleasurable. And you enjoy passing others more than you enjoy being passed by others. In your experience, you have learned that you are not likely to get a speeding ticket unless you are going more than 75MPH. Therefore, the antecedent that says "65MPH" actually means 75MPH in terms of behavior. That is what you have been taught by the consequences. But what would happen if tomorrow, on the same highway, you suddenly were stopped by a policeman and given a ticket for traveling at 75MPH? You would be shocked and angry. Yes, you know the speed limit is 65, but this isn't fair! It isn't "fair" because it is a change in the consequences. If every driver, every day, were given a ticket for traveling even 70 MPH, how long would it take for all the traffic to slow down to 65MPH?

What antecedents may work to promote studying by your child at home? One very powerful antecedent would be if one parent sat down with the child and read a book and suggested that they sit and read together. You do your homework, while the child does hers. Another antecedent would be saying, "OK, its homework time" and turning off the television.

But these will become effective if the child studies and then the parents provide a meaningful consequence, a positive consequence that the child will then associate with the antecedent. In other words, you sit and read with your child, and after fifteen minutes you say to the child, "I really like sitting here with you while we both read." That would be reinforcing to the child.

Imagine this situation, which is unfortunately too often typical. Mom, Dad, and their son are sitting after dinner watching *The Simpsons* on television. Ten minutes into the show Dad looks at his watch and says to his son, "Hey, Junior isn't it time for you get upstairs and do your homework?" (Prompt #1) His son does not answer and both keep watching the TV.

Ten minutes later a commercial comes on and Dad realizes that his son is still sitting there. "Hey, I thought I said it's time to get upstairs and do your homework," he says, a bit more aggravated this time. (Prompt #2) The son says, "OK, OK, I'm going; the shows almost over."

They both go back to watching TV. Ten minutes later the show is over and they are both sitting there watching the promos for the next show. Then Dad says to his son, "Hey, UPSTAIRS, NOW!" (Prompt #3) while pointing to the stairs. The son gets up and says, also in an aggravated voice "OK, OK, I'm going."

The way Dad is managing behavior in this situation is designed to teach his son NOT to respond to Prompts #1 and 2. He is teaching, but he doesn't realize what he is teaching. He is teaching his son that the only antecedent that he really needs to respond to is Prompt #3. Unfortunately, this teaches disrespect for authority, rather than respect. It teaches the son to wait for yelling and then respond with an angry tone of voice. This entire situation is completely unnecessary.

Your job is to redesign this behavior management situation. Your job is to create a situation in which the son learns, and it will take a few trials, to respond obediently to one prompt that is stated in a calm and dignified manner. Describe this new situation in terms of the ABC model. Be sure to make this a teaching experience by using positive reinforcement. Remember that you want him to learn to enjoy, to love, reading and learning. Discuss with your team why you think this will work.

Antecedent ⟹ **Behavior** ⟸ **Consequence**

_____

_____

_____

ANALYZING YOUR ANTECEDENTS

Let's do some analysis antecedents in your own work setting. Just look around, and I am sure you can see some. There are probably some as you walk into the building. Ask yourself whether or not these are effective. Why are they, or why are they not, effective?

When you think about the antecedents in your work environment, think about the graphs, charts, and process maps that may be visible. Do these serve to prompt the desired behavior? Do you think that the size and color of these may have any effect? How could you maximize their effect?

Antecedent	⟹	Behavior	⟸	Consequence

POSITIVE REINFORCEMENT AND THE 4 TO 1 RULE

Toyota practices 4 to 1. What does it mean and where does it come from? I'll let you in on a bit of motivational trivia. In 1973 I joined Aubrey Daniels and Fran Tarkenton in Atlanta where they had just started Behavioral Systems, Inc. The company was focused on spreading the use of positive reinforcement in industry. Around that time a behavioral psychologist named Dr. Ogden Lindsley did research in classrooms to determine what ratio of positive to negative comments by teachers resulted in the highest rate of learning by students. The answer: 3.57 to 1. Since we expected that no one would remember 3.57 to 1 (although this author has for some strange reason), we rounded it off to 4 to 1.

For several years we worked in southern textile miles teaching supervisors to "Catch Someone Doing Something Good Today" and we had them recording their own behavior of interactions with employees. How many of those interactions were positive and how many were negative? How many were recognizing good behavior and how many were criticizing bad behavior? Initially, most supervisors found that they were more likely to be 1 to 4, rather than 4 to 1, in other words, four times as negative as positive.

Every parent, and every manager, should know that punishing bad behavior may suppress that behavior, but if you don't reward the opposite good behavior; the child is likely to just misbehave in another way. We do what pays off in a positive way. You get what you reward! If you want good performance you must positively reinforce good behavior.

REINFORCING VALUES

How values are transmitted is very easily seen by understanding the ABC model. If you want your children to value reading and education, how do you transmit this as a value that will impact their behavior? Of course, you model reading behavior yourself (an antecedent). And, you praise and reinforce your child for doing the same (a consequence).

If you look at the next two pages, think about how we develop our values today and how we could tomorrow. Today, what are the antecedents that prompt the behavior to occur and what are the consequences (what happens) after the behavior has occurred. In the future if we want to reinforce positive behaviors what antecedents do we need to put in place and what consequences do we need to happen to make sure the positive behaviors get repeated?

There is nothing more important than values in any organization. Do we really value continuous improvement? Do we value innovation? Do we value teamwork and sharing knowledge? If we do value these or other values, how do we make them real in our organizations? On the following pages, identify what you think are the few most critical values for your team or organization. Analyze how we teach those values today, and how we could teach them in the future.

How We Do Reinforce Values Today		
Antecedent	**Behavior**	**Consequence**
Value 1:		
Value 2:		
Value 3:		
Value 4:		

How We Could Reinforce Values Tomorrow		
Antecedent	Behavior	Consequence
Value 1:		
Value 2:		
Value 3:		
Value 4:		

INTRINSIC AND EXTRINSIC REINFORCEMENT

There are several different ways to understand the different types of consequences that impact behavior. One way is to understand that some motivation comes intrinsically from the work itself. If you enjoy playing the piano or playing tennis, it isn't work. You don't need to be paid for this activity because it is intrinsically reinforcing. In almost every job there are elements of intrinsic reinforcement. The ability to improve performance is intrinsically reinforcing, the relationships with team members can make our work more intrinsically reinforcing. Novelty, changing tasks and learning new tasks, makes more work enjoyable.

Much of the work that needs to get done in this world is not sufficiently intrinsically motivating and requires extrinsic motivation. Extrinsic reinforcement is, of course, our compensation – both salary or wage, and bonuses. But, ordering pizza for your team because they achieved some performance goal, or taking them out to dinner, or an award of some type, are all extrinsic reinforcement.

Consider some of the activities that are critical to your work and consider what intrinsic and extrinsic reinforcement strengthens or maintains these activities.

Work Tasks or Behavior	Intrinsic Reinforcement	Extrinsic Reinforcement

TYPES OF CONSEQUENCES

There are three types of consequences to behavior. The first is positive reinforcement. The word "positive" doesn't refer to something you like. It refers to the *presentation*, rather than the *removal* of a reinforcing event. There is "negative" reinforcement, which does not mean punishment. It means the withdrawal of a stimulus that increases a performance. In all cases the word "reinforcement" is empirically defined by the increased frequency of a behavior. If there is no change in behavior, you cannot correctly say that you "reinforced" someone's

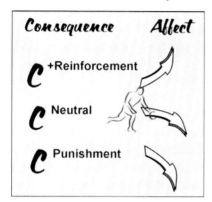

behavior. Similarly, you cannot say that you have "taught" someone if they have not learned. You can say "I tried to teach them," but whether they were taught or reinforced is determined by whether their behavior changed.

This empirical definition, determined by an actual change in frequency of behavior, may seem like an academic difference. But it is actually very important. It is part of becoming *fact based* in how we manage.

Positive reinforcement can be of many kinds. It can be social ("Thank you, I really appreciate your doing that for me!"); it can be material (a gift or money); it can be intrinsic.

There are also neutral consequences. This is when nothing happens. But nothing happening is a consequence in itself. Imagine that you have worked very hard on a report for your manager. You were told that this was an important study, so you worked at night and on the weekend to get it done. You believe that you did a great job, and you are very proud of the work you did. You then bring the report to your manager. He isn't in, but you lay it on his desk where he can't possibly miss it. A day goes by, and you hear nothing. A week goes by, and you hear nothing. A month goes by, and you hear nothing. What will be the effect on your behavior? This neutral consequence will de-motivate you. The rate of behavior will decline. The next time you are asked to do a similar job, you will be less excited, and it is likely that you will put in less effort. Your performance has gone down. This is the effect of neutral consequences.

We are all familiar with punishment. Punishment is the presentation of an event that reduces the rate or frequency of a behavior. Just as reinforcement is empirically defined by a change in the frequency of behavior, punishment is also empirically defined. Punishment is only punishment if the behavior occurs less frequently. It is very, very, common for parents to behave in a way that they think is punishing when it is actually doing nothing or even reinforcing a behavior. This can happen in the workplace also.

UNDERSTANDING THE SYSTEM OF CONSEQUENCES

In all organizations, there is a system of reinforcement or appreciation. In the society, there is a similar system. Why does government constantly change the tax code to provide a deduction for investments in oil drilling, or research, or education? Because tax deductions are a form of reinforcement, and the government uses this to strengthen effort in that direction.

Every school has a system of reinforcing good academic performance. Every sport has a scorekeeping system and a system to reinforce good performance in many ways. There is a Rookie of the Year Award, an award for the best lineman, the best quarterback, and the best special team player. There are hundreds of different types of reinforcers that are designed to reward many different kinds of behavior.

Choose a sport and ask yourself these questions:

How many different types of positive reinforcement can we name in either a college or professional sport (such as soccer, baseball, football, or basketball)? Make a list. What behavior is each designed to increase?

Reinforcement	Behavior
_____	_____
_____	_____
_____	_____
_____	_____
_____	_____

Why has it proven effective to have so many different types of positive reinforcement? Why not just rely on one?

The answer is that people are different. In sports you have different positions in which players are able to perform in different ways. A defensive lineman can do different things than the quarterback or a wide receiver. So to motivate all of them, there must be different kinds of measurement and different kinds of awards. Notice also in our sport that some of the awards are individual and some are team. Why is this important? If every player were only thinking about how he could win an individual award, this might work contrary to good teamwork. Similarly, in your own team environment you should have both individual and team recognition or reinforcement.

As a group exercise, it will be a good idea to share what you have come up with among your team members. Now ask yourself the question, what performance do we want to increase, and what types of reinforcement could be added that would improve that performance.

THE BALANCE OF CONSEQUENCES

The idea of a balance of consequences is that for every decision or behavior, there are likely to be consequences, both positive and negative, on both sides of the equation. Deciding to take job A or to take job B involves assessing the balance of consequences, potential rewards and potential negative events for either choice. Sometimes only a slight shift in the balance of consequences will tip the scale.

When we think about improving the performance of a team or an individual we can think about increasing some positive consequence for the desired behavior, or reducing some negative consequence, without feeling that we have to change all of the consequences. Whether we eat that pie and ice cream tonight will not be determined by eliminating all positive consequences. After all, it does taste good and that is reinforcing!! But, if we can add some reinforcement on the other side of the balance, for eating well and deferring gratification, we can change the behavior.

MAKING REINFORCEMENT EFFECTIVE

What are the keys to the effective use of positive reinforcement to improve individual or team performance?

SHAPE BEHAVIOR:

We don't learn a new language all at once. We learn it in small bites, each bite getting a bit larger and more complex than the previous one. We learn virtually everything, at least everything that is complex, by taking small steps that get larger and larger.

Reinforcing gradual improvement is called "shaping" behavior. Like a statue being made out of clay, it takes shape gradually, with repeated encouragement.

I remember when my second daughter was taking "keyboard" lessons and she called me into her room and said, "Daddy listen to this." It was Three Blind Mice, or something, but I couldn't really tell. It was an effort, but it was not exactly a concert performance. I could have said, "Well, that is not what I was hoping to get when I paid for those lessons. Call me when you can play something well!" If I had, this would have been the end of those lessons and probably any motivation for her to learn music. No! Daddy knows his job. Of course I said, "That's wonderful; it sounds like you are really learning some good songs!" and she smiled.

All parents know that you must reinforce approximations (shaping) toward a goal performance if you are going to motivate a child to learn. We are all the same. You and I need reinforcement for our efforts, for making improvement, for trying. A team will not instantly achieve its goals. But, it should be recognized for making improvement and for making the effort to improve. If it keeps trying to find improvement it will succeed.

DO IT IMMEDIATELY AND FREQUENTLY:

There is a lot of research that proves that the longer the delay, the less impact the reinforcement will have on strengthening a behavior it follows. If you reinforce immediately, the value of the reinforcement is greatest. Have you ever handed in work and waited months for feedback? When it came, you probably didn't feel any great joy.

Because immediacy matters, we need systems and habits of reinforcement that provide many opportunities for earning recognition or rewards. If there is only the monthly paycheck and an annual bonus or review, there are simply not enough opportunities to provide frequent and immediate reinforcement. Motivation depends on the immediacy and frequency of reinforcement.

PERSONALIZE IT:

What may be experienced as reinforcing by one person may not be by another. Some individuals may love to be recognized and applauded in a public gathering, while that same recognition may make others feel extremely uncomfortable. Some may consider time off from work a great reward while others would rather be rewarded with an additional assignment. Just as you think about the personal interests when buying a birthday present for someone, consider the personal interests of the individual you are encouraging in the work setting.

USE VARIETY:

We love variety in most aspects of our lives. If the same thing, words or events, are used repeatedly, they will become less meaningful. The best reinforcement is the surprise, delivered when least expected or spontaneously. Simply varying the schedule on which reinforcement is delivered can greatly increase overall performance with no additional costs.

You can vary both the type of reinforcement (what) and the schedule (when). The knowledge to vary both will significantly raise the effectiveness of your performance improvement efforts.

BE CONSISTENT:

A sense of fairness and justice results from the consistency with which reinforcement is delivered. Inconsistent use of reinforcement creates disunity. Consistency does not mean not varying reinforcement. It means providing equality of reinforcement to different people or at different times. Just as parents teach values by consistently approving behavior, managers teach values by the consistency in their expressions of appreciation. By rewarding improvement consistently, managers give members of the organization confidence in the values represented by that appreciation. With consistency come confidence and the elimination of fear. If employees can see that you are consistent in your approval or disapproval, they will come to trust that value.

STRENGTHENING BEHAVIOR WITHIN OUR TEAM

Let's try to apply the idea of positive reinforcement to improving behavior that we think is important.

TEAM BEHAVIOR			
WHAT BEHAVIOR MATTERS?	DOES IT NEED TO BE STRENGTHENED OR WEAKENED?	WHAT ARE THE CURRENT CONSEQUENCES?	WHAT REINFORCEMENT CAN BE STRENGTHENED?

ANALYZING HUMAN PERFORMANCE PROBLEMS

Many years ago, Robert Mager and Peter Pipe devised a model for analyzing performance problems, performance analysis, that is still extremely useful.[15] Whenever you observe a human performance problem, you can use this model to analyze the problem and define a solution.

The model essentially begins by asking the question – "Is it a **can't do** or **won't do** problem?" You will know this if you ask, "If his/her life depended on it, could he/she do it now?" If you ask me to sing opera, or play concert piano and you told me my life depended on it, I am dead! It isn't a "want to" issue. I just cannot do those things. It does not matter how big the reward or how big the threat, I simply don't have the skills. Maybe I could have developed these skills if my parents had trained me to sing or play golf at an early age, but it is unlikely even with training. I wasn't genetically endowed with the ability to sing opera. These are

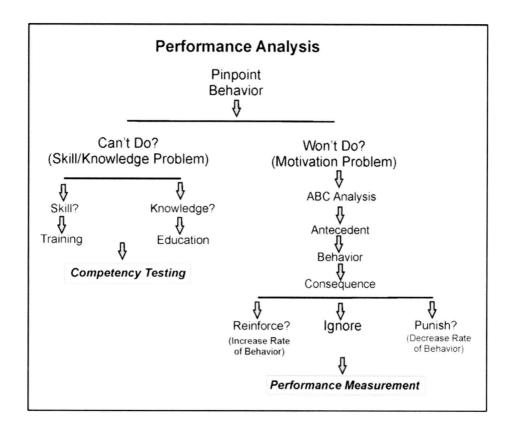

---

[15] Mager, Robert F. and Pipe, Peter. *Analyzing Performance Problems or You Really Oughta Wanna*. Atlanta, CEP Press, 1997.

"can't do" rather than "won't do" problems.

In the work setting, most "can't do" performance problems, problems of knowledge or skill, are not like singing opera. They don't require unusual genetic material, and they don't have to be developed in early childhood. They simply require training. This is true for most nursing and home support skills.

Many of the performance problems in a work setting are within the capability of employees; they just haven't been "made to matter" in a way that creates the necessary motivation.

If a problem is a "can't do" problem, it then requires the development of new skills through training, rather than motivation. If the problem is "won't do," a motivation problem, then the techniques of positive appreciation or positive reinforcement can strengthen that performance.

EXERCISE

With your team members, select one human performance problem. Work through the performance analysis model, and develop a solution to this problem. First, work through a 'can't do' problem. Be specific about what you would do, then work on a 'won't do' problem and again be specific about what you would do. Now, implement an improvement plan using this analysis.

CHAPTER 13

MAPPING YOUR VALUE STREAM

In this chapter your team will be guided to identify their "core" and "enabling" processes, map the value stream of those processes, and, initiate continuous improvement. Every team should be expert in their process and should be able to visualize the map of that process. This mapping is also at the heart of any kaizen event.

OBJECTIVES

1. To identify the work processes that are the responsibility of your team.

2. To learn methods of analyzing work processes to improve cycle time, reduce costs, and increase reliability and productivity.

THE VALUE IS IN THE FLOW

Continuous Improvement is about the flow of the work, from suppliers to customers, and creating the ideal flow that will add the most value for your customers and contain the least possible waste. The ideal process is so lacking in interruptions that it feels natural - it *flows*.

High performing teams or individuals appear *natural* when their performance flows with seemingly little effort. Athletes experience *flow*, or what they may call, "being in the zone." A musician may say she is in "the groove." Flow for an individual is complete focus, absorption in a task, when all energies move with ease and without interruption. Rather than feeling like great exertion, the work feels natural and exhilarating.

Mihaly Csikszentmihalyi described flow as the psychology of optimal experience. *"It is what the sailor holding a tight course feels when the wind whips through her hair, when the boat lunges through the waves like a colt – sail, hull, wind, and sea humming in a harmony that vibrates in the sailor's veins. It is what the painter feels when the colors on the canvas begin to set up a magnetic tension with each other, and a new thing, a living form, takes shape in front of the astonished creator."* [16]

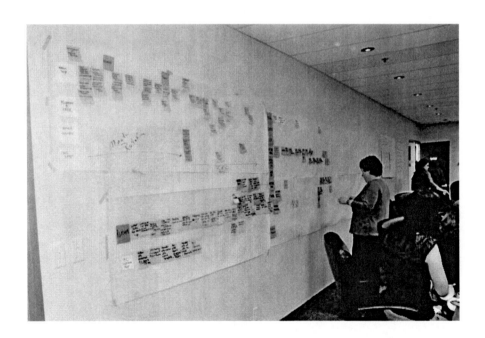

---

[16] Csikszentmihalyi, Mihaly. Flow: The Psychology of Optimal Experience. New York. Harper Perennial, 1990. p. 3.

If you have ever watched a great basketball team run the court on a fast break with each player having perfect confidence in the other, looking one way, and passing the ball another with certainty that the teammate will be there, and three quick passes around and over defenders ends in what looks like an effortless dunk through the hoop, you have observed flow.

Processes at work rarely provide a similar sense of exhilaration. Notice that processes that are exhilarating are without interruption, have an efficiency of no unnecessary steps, and those who are engaged in the process are in control.

Think about these three elements of flow: a) no interruptions; b) unnecessary steps, and c) the players being in control. Do you feel that the process that you perform every day incorporates these elements?

What Inhibits "Flow" in Our Process		
Elements of Flow	What Currently Inhibits Flow?	How Could We Improve Flow?
No Interruptions		
No Unnecessary Steps		
Players in Control		

In a high performing organization, the teams and structures are formed around the process to enable the process Customers pay for the output of the process, not any artificial requirement of vertical approvals or orders issued *up the line*. Why shouldn't the organization be ordered to serve the needs of the flow of the process, to support and enable the process, rather than the other way around?

Teams are formed and designed to optimize the ability of team members to control and manage their process. If you were designing the ideal organization, to create optimum flow in the process, you would design the team structure to optimize each team's capability to manage and improve their process. You would be sure to provide them with all the information they need to improve the process. You would be sure to provide all necessary tools, skills and knowledge, and the decision-making authority to so that the team members are empowered to make changes, experiment, and institute changes in standard work. And, you would provide positive reinforcement for improvements in performance.

DEATH BY PROCESS!

Processes can kill you and sometimes do. I don't know how many coroners' reports have said "Death by Process," but many should have.

My consultants and I were working with a large health care provider in the Midwest and had been given the assignment to "re-engineer" the core process in the organization. Of course, the core process was providing health care solutions to individuals in both clinics and hospitals. A design team was formed to study the core process and develop an improved solution to eliminate many well-known problems. The seriousness of those problems was sometimes buried under the routine of daily work.

The design team, after several months of work analyzing the process and developing a solution, made a presentation to the senior Executive Committee that included the company president. Because they were about to propose some fairly radical solutions, they were concerned that they get the executives' attention in a dramatic way. So, they dramatized a patient experience. They role-played a scenario in which one of their members develops an unexplained stomach pain.

Her first stop is to her general practitioner and after filling out forms and sitting for an hour in the waiting room, she is told that she needs to see a specialist and is given a list of several specialists whom she could then call.

Of course, she has taken off from work for her first appointment.

She goes home and gets on the phone. It will be a month before any of the specialists can see her. She makes an appointment.

She shows up a month later at the specialist's office. The specialist immediately tells her that he wants her to take a series of tests and she is referred to a clinic that provides the necessary tests. She calls and makes an appointment for two weeks later.

When she shows up at the clinic, she is informed that she has to get pre-approval from her insurance provider before they can administer these tests.

She goes home and calls the insurance provider.

You get the picture. The story was detailed and frustrating to just listen to, let alone if you had to live through it. The story ends, after months of wrong appointments, delays, and re-routing, in the doctor's office where she finds out that she has cancer and the doctor informs her that treatment could have been much more successful if she had come in sooner. She dies. In effect, *the process* murdered her.

The leader of the design team, to lighten up the somewhat somber mood in the meeting with the executives said, "Of course that story may be a bit exaggerated. Perhaps we don't kill people, but people do suffer through our system."

With that the president of the company, a doctor and healthcare executive for many years, interrupts. "Excuse me, but there is nothing exaggerated about that. That was my mother! That is exactly what happened to my mother."

A long and tense silence followed as everyone tried to figure out how to respond to that revelation. The president broke the silence and said, "Well, let's fix it!" Not surprisingly, they approved implementation of the redesigned process.

Isn't it odd that we handle packages with more efficiency and care than we handle patients? And that is because package delivery companies have become much more focused on eliminating waste from their processes and assuring that their process meets their customer's requirements.

Mapping Your Process

How we think and feel about process improvement is just as important as any specific technique. Dr. Deming famously said that "95% of quality problems are in the process, not the person. But 95% of the time we blame the person and fail to improve the process. Then we wonder why we still have the problem." This is a profound bit of wisdom at the heart of process improvement.

Discuss each of the following attitudes of process improvement with your team. Do you and your team mates adhere to these attitudes?

The Attitudes of Process Improvement:

- MOST PROBLEMS ARE IN THE PROCESS, NOT THE PERSON!
- DON'T BLAME THE PERSON - FIX THE PROCESS.
- EVERY PROCESS CAN BE IMPROVED – FOREVER!
- PROBLEMS ARE NORMAL – EACH AN OPPORTUNITY TO LEARN.
- MEASUREMENT OF PROCESSES LEADS TO IMPROVEMENT.
- EVERY PROCESS MUST HAVE A "PROCESS OWNER" OR TEAM RESPONSIBLE FOR ITS EXECUTION AND IMPROVEMENT.
- WE "KNOW WHAT WE ARE DOING" BY KNOWING THE PROCESS.

Managers today are a hundred times more aware of their processes than they were twenty years ago. The Toyota Production System, what we now like to call lean management, is an innovation in process. It is not an innovation in either product or service. It is all about the effectiveness of the process of making cars that led to tremendous competitive advantage for Toyota and other car companies. FEDEX, McDonald's, Facebook and Ebay are all examples of companies built on a breakthrough in process innovation. These companies didn't create a unique product or service that had never been done before. Ebay is essentially a store, a flea market, a way to buy and sell. We have done that for thousands of years. But, it is an innovation in process that makes it easier for millions of people to buy and sell from their home.

Process thinking becomes a way of life. Process thinking is learning to look horizontally through the organization as work flows. Those who are trained in lean processes can walk through a work setting and immediately see piles that signify process delays, interruptions in the form of pallets or in-boxes on the desk, or hear questions about "who owns the problem," all of which indicate process problems. You should work on developing your automatic, habitual thoughts about process. Developing this competence will serve you well. Think flow!

DIFFERENT TYPES OF PROCESSES MAPS

A process is a set of related activities that together result in a desired output for a customer.

A lean process is one in which every step adds value, speed through the process is optimized, there are no interruptions or re-work, and those who work in the process seek continuous improvement.

The set of activities that comprise a process can simply be listed on a sheet of paper. However, we have all heard the saying that a picture is worth a thousand words. It is true. If you have ever downloaded directions on MapQuest, or used a GPS in your car, you received a list of turns and highways. You then also see the map of the suggested route. The map is much more helpful. Human beings were created as visual creatures. We like to see pictures, and we find it easier to understand a picture than a list of words.

You will have to decide the most useful way to map your process. It will be helpful to look at a number of different process maps and see how each may be useful in different situations.

MACRO MAPS

Let's start with a very high level map. Think of "macro maps" as looking at your organization from an airplane thirty thousand feet in the air. They give you the big picture.

The following is a macro map of a large manufacturing and marketing company and how the leadership team drew their major processes. Once the team and the CEO agreed that "this is what we do", the restructured the senior team so that the leader of each of these major processes was a member of the leadership team.

WORK PROCESS MAPS

Your team is more likely to be concerned with a more detailed description of how you do your daily work. A map that describes the work we do is a work process map. Again, there are many different ways to map work processes, so it will help to look at a few examples.

The following is a very simple map created by a team responsible for managing a conference. You will see that they have identified the major core activities across the top. This was their first map of their process. Then, they decided that more detail would be needed so they "drilled down" and mapped the detailed steps within each of the original general steps. You can see that under "define customers, needs and goals" they have mapped the five steps for getting that job done. Of course, they did this for each of the seven steps.

One of the advantages of doing this is that this team plans and manages a conference each year. In the past, every time they had to plan a conference, they would have new members who had not done it before. So the learning would begin again with little or no memory of the lessons of previous years. Now, at the beginning of their planning for the conference they take out the planning map and review the steps from last year. They decided whether these steps still make sense this year, and they assign responsibility for each of the steps. Then, after that conference is completed, they have a learning-reflection meeting. They review what went well and what did not go well. They look at the map again and make changes so the team next year can avoid any mistake they made. In this way, each annual team is able to improve the process and maintain some "corporate memory." This is a form of knowledge management that is often lacking in organizations.

IDENTIFYING THE "VALUE" IN THE PROCESS STREAM

Another name for process mapping is value stream mapping. What is the meaning of "value?" Value is created when there is a transformation in the material, information, or other input, and that transformation is necessary to satisfy the customer. Anything that does not add value is waste. Sitting still is waste. Re-doing is waste. Any time spent that is not directly creating the desired transformations is waste. The job of the team studying a process is to identify exactly which time, materials, motions, etc., are adding value and which are waste.

Value adding and non-value adding activity can be identified on your process map by using data boxes. Below you will see an example. These data boxes illustrate three measures of value: CT, the actual cycle time from beginning to the end of that process step; VCT, the value adding cycle time; and CTVR the ratio of value adding to total cycle time.

Identifying the actual cycle time and the value adding time requires discipline, doing your homework. You should not guess. Go and see! Go and measure! Get the data. Often, it will surprise you.

Below you will see a completed analysis of cycle time for one process. The total and value-adding cycle time of each step has been identified, as well as the totals for the overall process. The percent of value adding time is 12.7%. This is not an unusual ratio when processes are studied carefully. You will see that this team has set an ambitious goal of getting to 50% value adding time. This will mean eliminating a lot of non-value adding activity, delays, re-do loops, or other interruptions in the process.

Which value measures you decide to use when analyzing your process will be dependent on the nature of the work and the output of the work. Beginning with cycle time, analysis is one of the most certain ways to get started.

COMMON PROCESS OR VALUE MEASURES

- CT = Cycle Time
- VCT=Value Adding Cycle Time
- CTVR=Ratio of Value Adding to Total Cycle Time
- CO=Change Over Time
- No.O=Number of Separate Operations
- WT=Work Time (actual value adding work)
- TT=Total Time Worked or Assigned to an Operation
- SC=Scrap
- SCR=Scrap rate (ratio of scrap to total)
- I=Inventory

You decide what process measures are most important for your process!!!

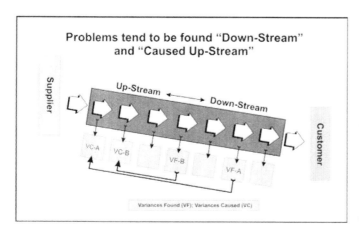

Problems tend to be found "Down-Stream" and "Caused Up-Stream"

Another useful question to ask when analyzing processes is, "where are problems found, and where are they caused?" It is normal that problems are caused in one place, but discovered in another place. This almost always means that they are caused "upstream" and found "downstream." For example, imagine that you are making chairs. One department cuts and prepares legs for assembly. A "downstream" department does the actual assembly. It is important that the legs are exactly the same length. Hopefully, those who are cutting the legs are conducting their own self-inspection. However, it will not be surprising if those who are assembling the chair find that some of the legs are irregular and cause the chair to wobble. In such cases it is important that there be a clear feedback loop established whereby the assembly team can immediately provide feedback upstream to the team that caused the problem. This feedback loop should be almost instantaneous to avoid the production of off-specification parts. Any delay in this feedback loop will increase waste of materials and time.

RELATIONSHIP MAPS (WHO DID WHAT?)

The following is a very simple map. This is a process with which we are all familiar. It is a simple work process: making a meal. If you are a good cook (like me!) you know that the order in which you do things is very important. For example, if you are going to make a spaghetti dinner, you don't start your preparations by sticking the pasta in a pot of cold water, and then thinking about how to prepare the sauce. You begin preparing the sauce long before putting water on to boil for the spaghetti. Order is important in most work processes. It is one of the reasons why you should map your processes. Problems often occur because the order is wrong. Or you have missed a step or have unnecessary steps.

1. Invite guests to dinner.
2. Decide on the menu.
3. Go shopping.
4. Cut the onions and brown.
5. Add and brown meat.
6. Cut and add green pepper and mushrooms.
7. Add tomato sauce.
8. Add spices.
9. Simmer for two hours.
10. Make salad.
11. Cook vegetable.
12. Warm water to boil.
13. Set table.
14. Add spaghetti to water.
15. Rinse spaghetti.
16. Serve above.
17. Eat.
18. Clean table.
19. Wash dishes.

While this process map is useful, it is also lacking a lot of very helpful information. Who is doing what? Why is one person doing something and not other people? Does one person bear too much responsibility or not enough?

It is much easier to find answers to these questions in a "relationship map." The following map contains exactly the same steps; it is the same process, as the previous one. But, now you have who is doing what. You can see that Dad is doing the majority of the work. Maybe he wants it this way, or maybe he doesn't, but it certainly raises some questions that should be asked. You can see that relationship problems are often created by how we do things, the relationships reflected in the process. What problems do you think this process might lead to? You might try reversing the roles of Mom and Dad. Do you like it better or worse that way? Why?

Before you start mapping your processes it is important to agree on what symbols you will use. There is no rule or religion to this. The following is a set of symbols you can use, but you can choose others also. Just agree on them. That is what is important. You may find it helpful to use symbols that you find in a software program such as Visio. The most recent version of MS Word includes symbols for process mapping.

HOW TO TURN PROCESSES INTO FLOW

Here are some simple steps to follow to create a process map.

1. CLARIFY PURPOSE AND GOALS

The purpose and goals of every process should be clear. You have may have already done this. Just review them here. The purpose should make clear why the process is important and to whom. The goals should not be detailed scorecard goals, but the general goal of the process.

2. AGREE ON RESPONSIBILITY

Is the process the responsibility of the entire team, more than one team, or just a few members of the team? The process should be defined by those who "own" the process. Who owns this process?

3. DEFINE INPUTS & OUTPUTS

If you have completed the work in the previous chapters, you have already done much the necessary work to be ready to work on process improvement. You should have answers to the following questions

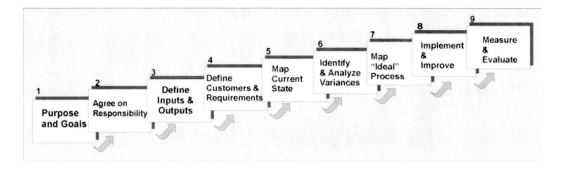

- What are the inputs to your work process (include materials, information, capital, people)? What are the requirements for each of these inputs?

- Who are the suppliers who provide input? What capabilities are needed on the part of suppliers in order to meet these requirements?

- What are the feedback loops from your team to your suppliers, and how do they function (speed, quality of information)?

- What are the outputs of your work system?

- Given the above, what are the requirements for your work process?

- What are the feedback loops that inform us of customer satisfaction, and how do they function (speed, quality of information)?

4. DEFINE CUSTOMER REQUIREMENT

If you followed the guidance in the previous chapters, you have this. It is helpful to just put this on a flip chart so the team can see and refer to these requirements as they begin mapping the process.

5. MAP THE CURRENT STATE

It is a mistake to start mapping how you think things should be until you have mapped how things actually get done today. This is the "current state" of the process.

It is often true that even people doing the job don't know how the whole process gets done. People only understand their very narrow piece of the work. You can't analyze how things can be improved or study the causes of variances if you don't know how things are currently done. First, map the current state of the process.

It may be helpful to imagine a meeting in which a team is going to map their process. Let's go through how that meeting might flow:

✓ First, let's check to see that we have the right people in the room. Are the team members in this room the "world's greatest experts" in this process? Is there anyone else we should invite to participate in mapping the process?

✓ Now let's define the process. Do we agree on the process boundaries? Where does this process begin and where does it end?

✓ Now we will make a list of the inputs and outputs and customer requirements for this process. We will also make a list of any other specifications for the output of this process.

✓ Now let's map the current state steps in the process. Let's start this by brainstorming without worrying about whether we have the steps in exactly the right order. It is very helpful to have Post-It-Notes, especially the 3x5 kind. Have the team members write down steps in the process and put those on the wall. It is very helpful to have a roll of brown paper that you can spread across the wall. Give yourself lots of room.

✓ Some process steps are work activities; some are decisions. If you can, use a different color for these. Or you can indicate in some way that these are symbols. Agree on another kind of note for delays.

✓ Give everyone a chance to get all of the steps up on the wall and then ask, "Who are the Players in the process?" Make a note for each individual who participates in the work of this process. Now put these players in a vertical column to the left of your paper. If you can, draw a horizontal line across the paper, representing the occasions when that player may be involved.

✓ Now order the steps. Arrange each of the work steps and decisions on your map going from left to right. They should be in chronological order. If two things are happening at the same time, they can be on top of each other. If they happen after one another, then they should be to the right of the previous step.

✓ Ask yourself how these happen in time. Are there delays between steps? If these delays are for any significant amount of time, put a post-it-note up for that delay.

✓ Now create a timeline from left to right. It may be that the process is not the same every time. Take a typical process cycle for the sake of your studying the process. On the left, when the process begins, put a zero at the beginning of your timeline. Then, at the end of the process put the amount of time a typical cycle takes, whether it is one hour or one month. Then, try to put time marks from left to right as the steps occur. This will give you some idea where the delays are occurring and how much time is involved in each step of the process. This may raise some questions when you analyze the process for speed or cycle time improvement.

✓ This is probably enough work for one meeting. Getting to this point may have taken one to several hours. When a team is assigned to work on a complex process that flows through the organization, just mapping the current state may involve many meetings over a period of weeks. It may also be necessary to go and interview other people who are working in the process in order to have knowledge of those steps.

✓ It is sometimes desirable at this point to invite others into the meeting, perhaps some managers, perhaps members of other teams and ask them if they agree that this is how things currently work. They may have some insights that your team may have missed.

✓ It will probably be in another meeting that you begin to analyze the variances in the process. Below is an introduction to the analysis of variances. This will be explored in more detail in the following chapter.

6. IDENTIFY AND ANALYZE VARIANCES:

A variance is anything in a process that varies from the way things should ideally be done or a result that varies from customer requirements. The next chapter will deal in more depth with analyzing variances.

For now, you should be aware that your process may include any single one, or a combination of at least five different kinds of problems or variances. You have "waste" in the form of unnecessary steps, unnecessary motions within a step, or waste in the form of delays that could be eliminated. Any step that doesn't add value to the process is also "waste."

6

Identify & Analyze Variances

You may also have a cycle time variance from what may be an ideal cycle time. Speed is an important factor in almost all competition these days. Think about the pit stop in an auto race. Speed matters, and anything that slows down the movement from input to output should be questioned.

Probably the most obvious variance will be a variance from specifications. Your team should be able to measure conformance to specifications at each step in the process and at the end of the process.

Work teams and management teams are managing a business. Imagine that your team is actually a separate company with its own revenue and its own costs. You are now responsible for managing the business. If it was your business, you would seek to eliminate any unnecessary costs and costs that do not add value to the output of the team.

And, finally, you will want to ask yourself whether or not your process conforms to your principles. Look back on the principles you established in a previous chapter. If you have a principle to be customer focused, is your process genuinely customer focused? If you have principles to make decisions at the lowest possible level in the organization, does your process conform to that principle?

7. MAP THE "IDEAL" PROCESS

There is no such thing as an ideal process. There is only the most ideal process we can imagine at this time. That ideal will change as we experiment and learn more about our process. But for now, map what you regard to be the ideal process. Start where input comes into the organization and the first step is taken. Go through all the steps you would recommend for a future process. Be sure not to add back in waste or sources of variance that you have eliminated.

8. IMPLEMENT AND IMPROVE

If you have followed all of the steps above, it is now time to implement your new and improved process. However, you may feel that you have more work to do to analyze problems in the process. If this is the case, the next couple of chapters will help you find and make those improvements. Finding improvement and implementing those improvements should be an ongoing process, something you do many times in a year. By finding and implementing improvements to your process, you are doing your job as a high performance team.

9. MEASURE AND EVALUATE

If you have developed your team scorecard, you have identified measures of your work process. These are measures that you should be graphing and monitoring on a daily or weekly basis. The improvements you have made in your process should be reflected in these scores.

CHAPTER 14

ANALYZING VARIANCES

A variance is a problem. It is something that varies from either the standard way of doing things, or from performance that meets the customer's expectations. In other words, it is a problem. The purpose of this chapter is to analyze your work process to eliminate waste and discover causes of quality, productivity and cost problems.

OBJECTIVES:

1. To understand the costs and causes of variation.

2. To study variation within our own core work process and seek to reduce variation.

If you are to become a truly lean organization you must become process focused and must continually seek to reduce or eliminate variances.

There is statistical variation and there is a variance from how things could ideally be done. Both are problems within a process, and both need to be the focus of attention by your team.

Statistical variation is the variability around a mean for any performance. There is always some variation around a mean. The question is when is that a problem?

To understand variability it will help to understand a simple example. You may have a gun that you aim at a target. Let's assume that you are one hundred meters away from that target. Let's also assume that there is no wind and the gun is in a vice-grip so it will not move. Will every bullet land in exactly the same spot, assuming that the gun itself is perfectly stable? They will not all fall in the same place. If you fire fifty shots from the gun, you will see a pattern. That pattern illustrates the statistical variation resulting from this system. This pattern describes system performance. There is always variability around a mean. The average bullet may fall at or very close to the target, but the pattern will be in a circle around that point. Depending on the gun, (and how far back you are) the pattern may be a few centimeters wide or a few meters. This pattern will describe the capability of this system in its current state.

Knowing *system capability* and normal *system performance* is important knowledge for anyone managing any system. It is particularly important for anyone working with equipment or repeatedly producing a product.

COMMON AND SPECIAL CAUSES OF VARIATION

Dr. Deming described the important distinction between what he called *"common cause"* and *"special cause"* of variation. In the example of the bullets hitting a target, if you fire fifty or one hundred shots, you will see that all of the shots fall within some circle. This variation from the mean, the center of the circle, is *common cause*. In other words, it is inherent in the nature of the system. The gun is a system with inputs, a process, and an output. The variability, under stable conditions (the gun is clean, it is not moving, etc.) that results from this system is common cause. Within the normal performance of this system, the only explanation for each variation is simple randomness. There is always random variability around a mean. Every system produces variation that describes the capability of that system. You can and should expect it. If you want to reduce this variation, reduce the size of the circle made by the bullets, you will have to change the system. You could add a longer barrel on the gun and that would probably reduce the variation.

This is an important understanding because if you know what normal performance for a system is, you won't blame the person operating within that system. Blaming individuals is useless. The system has to be redesigned.

But, there is another kind of variation and this is not the result of the inherent properties of the system. A *special cause* is the result of something "being wrong" in the operation of the system. In other words, if the circle on the target is normally a radius of twelve centimeters, this is "system" performance. However, if suddenly a bullet falls two meters away from the center, you know that this is not normal for this system. You only know this because you already have data on system performance. You immediately say "Hey, something is wrong here!" And what you mean is that "Hey, this is not a common cause; this is a special cause of variation." This is caused by some abnormality in the system or abnormal input. Now you can brainstorm the possible causes of this defect. The cause may be a bad bullet. Or something may have knocked and moved the gun. The gun may be getting dirty. There may be many possible reasons for a special cause.

The important point of this distinction is that you will do different things depending on whether the variation is a special or common cause variation. If you seek to improve the normal variation produced by a system, common cause, you will have to redesign that system. On the other hand, if you are witnessing a special cause, you would be making a serious mistake to redesign the system. This would cause even more variation. You need to track down the reason you have experienced a special cause.

What Performance Demonstrates Statistical Variability		
What is the Performance?	What is Normal System Performance?	What are Examples of Common and Special Cause

THE COST OF VARIATION

There is a cost to variation. For example, when you drive to work each day it may take an average of thirty minutes to make the drive from home to work. But, it is rarely exactly thirty minutes. It may vary ten minutes on either side. If the weather and traffic are good, you may get to work in twenty minutes. But if there is an accident, it could take a lot more than thirty minutes. Let us assume that you live in an area where there is a lot of road construction and there tend to be a lot of accidents. When there is no traffic and no construction, the process of driving from home to work is "interruption free." But, in your situation, during a normal drive to work, there is a fair likelihood of an interruption, something that will cause a deviation from the mean.

Now let's also assume that there are some consequences for being either late or early. Your team cannot start work until you get there. If one person is late by thirty minutes, that is the equivalent of all ten members of the team being late. The consequence is that there are three hundred minutes of lost work time. Being on time is so important that it is a factor in your performance reviews. If you are late too many times, that may result in not achieving a merit increase in pay. This is a risk that you do not want to take. On the other hand, if you are thirty minutes early, the door is locked and you can't enter. This means standing out in the cold. These are the costs of variation in the process. Variation almost always has costs even if we fail to see or understand them. We often behave on the assumption of variability in a process and we therefore consider it "just the way things are."

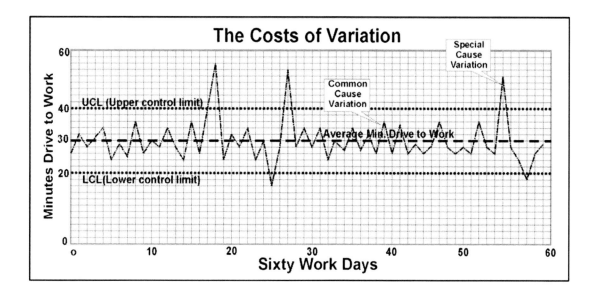

If you look at the above graph, you can see this variation illustrated. You have measured the time it takes you to drive to work for sixty days. The average is thirty minutes, but on three occasions it took about fifty minutes. On two occasions it took less than twenty minutes. Now that you know about the consequences of extreme variation (defining extreme as above or below the control limits), would you alter your behavior? What are the costs associated with this variation?

_____

_____

_____

_____

Now think about your own work process. Look at your most important three or four measures of performance. Do you know how these measures vary from day to day or by any other time frame? Make a graph of this variation? What are the costs of this variation? What are the causes?

_____

_____

_____

_____

_____

_____

_____

You are probably familiar with cause-and-effect or fishbone diagrams. These serve the simple purpose of stimulating brainstorming. It is important that your team look at variation in your process and seek to understand the causes of that variation. It would be a good idea to place this diagram on a flip chart and brainstorm the causes of variation in your work process. The points on the diagram are simply suggestions. You may have other, or more important, major causes.

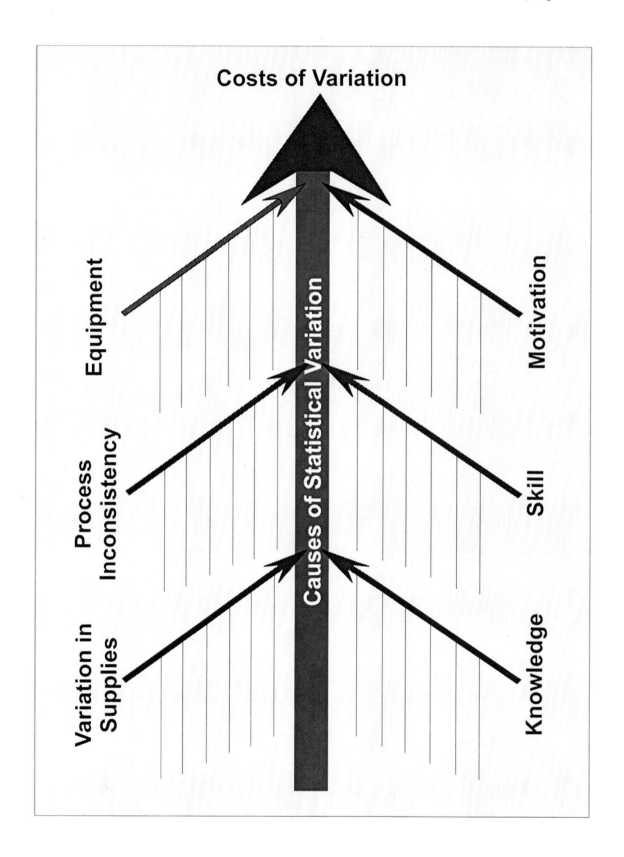

Variance Analysis Worksheet

Key Variance	Cause	Where it's Found	Who Controls	Solutions: Change Process, Supply, Tools, Human Performance

VARIATION WITHIN HUMAN PERFORMANCE

The examples given above are oriented to the manufacturing setting. Many teams using this manual will not be making "things" but will be involved in a service delivery process. In what is often called "knowledge work," the rate and process of work is much more independently controlled by the individual. For example, if you are creating advertising, you cannot define exactly how each creative process is going to proceed as if it was a repetitive process such as one on an assembly line. It may be that the best creative work may be watching television or taking a walk around the block to get ideas. If you are writing grant proposals, each proposal will require some different information and will require unique research and writing. When one understands the actual work involved, one is in a better position to judge the nature of the variation.

Variation is often a result of interaction with the uncontrollable events in the environment. Imagine a football team. Even if the team played the same opponent with the same players every game, there would still be some variation in performance. The quarterback would not throw the same number of completed passes each game. But in the real world, every opponent is different, with different defensive schemes, and this will cause variation in the play of the quarterback. You can think of the job of the defense as doing everything they can to create "variances" in the play of the quarterback.

Much of our work is like this, continually adjusting to the customer, the economic conditions, and competitors. The trick is to learn what forces are influencing performance, seek to control those we can control, and adjust to those we cannot control.

Selling is also a human performance process that is very much under the control of the individual, but also continually interacts with forces in the environment. How does the idea of variation apply to these types of human performance?

In the chart below you will see the annual performance for a team of new car salesman in a group of auto dealerships. **This is a "cumulative" graph. That means that each data point is added to the previous data points, so it never goes down. You will see that for the year the sales team will sell approximately one thousand automobiles.** That does not mean that each month they will sell exactly one twelfth of this number. If they sold exactly the same amount each month, all end of month sales points would be on the line that is on the slope from zero to one thousand. You will also notice that within each month there is a pattern. Sales vary from the first week of the month to the last week. In fact, in every case, the last week of the month has much stronger sales than the first week of the month. If you were the manager of this organization, it would probably benefit you to know why there is this variation in performance. What do you think is causing this end of month increase in sales?

You will also notice that if you take the maximum slope that occurs during the last week of the month and project this line, it is a significantly greater rate of performance than the average performance for the year.

The curve of performance within each month is what is known as a "scallop." It is very familiar to experimental psychologists who study the science of human behavior, particularly what are called "schedules of reinforcement." The sales people in this organization are very clearly on what is called a fixed-interval schedule of reinforcement. What this simply means is the rewards are delivered at the end of each month. After the end of each month, these salespeople experience what is known as a "post-reinforcement-pause." These sales people receive a monthly bonus check for their sales during the previous month. They receive this on the first day of the month. They do what most people do: as the potential reward approaches, they work harder to get that reward. We have all done this. It is the same as cramming the night before for the test in school. Congress passes the largest number of bills just before they achieve the reward of going home at the end of the session.

If you are a customer, what does this tell you about when is the best time to buy a car? When are you likely to get the best deal? You may not be surprised to know that it is during the last few days of the month. The incentive system conditions the sales people, and the sales people condition the customers to buy at the end of the month.

Understanding this pattern of variability and its cause can be extremely valuable to the organization. How could the reward system be modified to reduce the variability and increase the total sales? The answer is in shifting from a fixed-interval (once a month on the last day of the month) reward schedule, to one that varies and has the element of surprise, like all gambling that maintains strong and consistent rates of behavior.

What are processes and performance that are more the result of human motivation than the design of the process?

_____

_____

If you plot that performance on a graph, what variation will you see?

_____

_____

What are the causes of this variation?

_____

_____

CHAPTER 15

FINDING AND ELIMINATING WASTE

The purpose of this chapter is to engage in systematic and continuous efforts to eliminate all non-value adding activity, materials, time or costs from your processes. Eliminating waste has been a cornerstone of the Toyota Production System and whether in manufacturing, in service delivery, or in management processes, we should continually be looking for and eliminating waste.

OBJECTIVES:

1. To understand and identify the seven forms of waste in your work and organization.

2. To practice and implement waste elimination from your processes.

3. To understand and eliminate the six forms of management waste.

Just off the top of your head – what activities, time, or materials have you seen wasted in your organization? Make a quick list of the types of waste you have observed and what you think may be the causes of that waste.

Identify Waste	
Types of Waste	**Causes of Waste**

For more than forty years, Toyota has worked to improve the process of designing and building cars by focusing on the elimination of waste. They are still doing it today. For how long have you been eliminating waste from your processes? When will you be done?

Contrary to the understanding of many, the primary focus of improvement in lean organizations has not been making more money or managing quality, although both have been the result. The primary driver for improvement has been the elimination of waste. It is not the same as cost reduction!

Most companies cut costs, which usually mean cutting people, and they leave the waste. The waste is in the process, not the person. If you eliminate the waste in the process, you can then redeploy the person and other assets to "value-adding" work and thereby increase value to customers or customers. Company after company has gone out of business cutting costs, which results in worse products, worse service, fearful employees who lose their creativity, and the inevitable loss of customers. You stay in business by maximizing value to customers.

WHAT IS WASTE?

Any activity that does not directly contribute to providing excellent service delivery or producing your product is waste.

The founders of Lean Manufacturing were Taichi Ohno and Dr. Shigeo Shingo. They focused on seven types of waste:

1. **Inventory:** Any "piles" are waste. Anything that is standing still and not in motion is waste, whether it is in a warehouse or in bins or on pallets in the production area. Inventory consumes space (waste), requires employees to move and manage (waste), inventory requires accounting (waste), and instead of having one mistake that is caught immediately, you will have a large pile of defects... big waste! Just-in-time is the process of arranging the supply chain and production process so that each input arrives at the process just in time, and each output goes directly to the next stage of the process, just in time.

2. **Motion:** Motion is a key variable addressed by industrial engineering. Teams in lean processes constantly study their motions to determine how motions can be eliminated or made easier by placement of fax machines and filing cabinets.

3. **Transportation:** If steps in the process are separated by physical space, forklifts, trucks, dollies, or other mechanisms of transportation are required. All of this is waste. The production process should be designed to minimize transportation.

4. **Defects:** Every defective product is waste. The time, effort, and supply that went into producing it are waste. Re-working errors is necessary, but waste is not, because if it had been done right the first time, the re-work would not be needed. It is the job of the team to use problem-solving methods to study and eliminate waste.

5. **Waiting time:** Kanban and other methods in lean production are designed to eliminate waiting time. People should be flexible, trained, and assigned to move from one job to another in a production area so they can smooth the flow of production elements to prevent waiting for someone else to do something that only he or she can do.

6. **Overproduction:** Overproduction produces the need for storage, big piles rather than small piles.

7. **Processing:** By processing Shingo is referring to inefficiencies within a process – things done the wrong way, lack of training, etc.

Norman Bodek tells a Shingo story that may help us understand the attitude of eliminating waste in his excellent book Kaikaku.[17] Norman used to put on "Productivity" conferences at which I spoke for many years. These should have been called Lean conferences, but that term had not been invented yet. His conferences usually include talks by one of the masters of lean manufacturing and Quality Management, as well as lesser folks like me. Norman made trips to Japan and made it his mission to translate and bring to the United States the lessons from these innovators.

This story is from one of the trips to the U.S. he arranged for Dr. Shingo.

On Dr. Shingo's first visit to America I took him to a Dresser, Inc. manufacturing plant, where they were producing gasoline fuel dispensing systems. After first meeting the management team we walked around the plant floor with a small group of engineers and managers.

Dr. Shingo stopped in front of a punch press. He asked us all to look at the operation and to tell us the percentage of *value*

[17] Bodek, Norman. Kaikaku: The Power and Magic of Lean. PCS Press, Vancouver Washington, 2004.

adding time. He then took out his stopwatch to time the operation.

We watched two workers in front of the punch press bend down and pick up a large sheet of thin stainless steel from the left side of the press. They placed the steel into the bed of the press. Then they removed their hands to press buttons outside the press, which indicated that their hands were out and clear of the press. The large press came down and formed the metal into a side of a gasoline pump. Then the two workers reached into the press, removed the formed sheet and placed the formed sheet at the right side of the press.

Dr. Shingo asked, "What was the value adding percentage?"

One engineer said "100%; the workers never stopped working."

Another engineer said "75%," and another said "50%."

Dr. Shingo laughed and looked at his stop watch. "Only 12% of the time was the process adding value. Adding value is only when the dies are pressing against the metal to create a formed sheet. The rest of the time is waste."

Dr. Shingo then asked, "What can be done to increase the percent of value adding time?"

An engineer immediately said, "You can place a table over here and put the raw inventory sheets on top of the table. This would help the workers. They wouldn't need to bend down. They could just slide the sheets directly into the press."

Another engineer said, "We could install a leveler to automatically raise the sheet metal to keep it at a constant height, similar to what you might see in a cafeteria when you reach for a dinner plate."

A third engineer said, "We could put a spring into the back of the punch press to force the formed metal to leap forward after the stamping."

Dr. Shingo laughed and said, "Yes, you all know what to do, so do it!"

An important point to notice in this story is that Dr. Shingo did not TELL them anything to do. He merely asked the right questions and defined things as they really are. He knew waste when he saw it. This is the primary characteristics of managers in lean operations. They ask the right questions. They constantly seek to improve by eliminating waste. Also notice that Shingo never suggested that there was anything wrong with the workers or that they weren't working hard enough. He did not blame the person; he assumed the problem was in the process.

How do the seven forms of waste appear in your organization? They are generally described in terms of making a product. But think creatively and try to identify examples of each of these forms of waste in the service delivery or other processes at your organization.

The Seven Forms of Waste	
Type of Waste	**Examples in Your Organization**
Inventory	
Motion	
Transportation	
Defects	
Waiting Time	
Over Production	
Processing	

The concept of "value-adding" is important. It is the activity and time that actually adds value to the customer. The customer doesn't care how many motions the workers go through, how much they have to move stuff, store stuff, or rework stuff. That all just adds cost. If your manager told you to go run around the building five times, you might do it. You might get paid during that time, and you might call it "work." But what value did it add for the customer? None!

ELIMINATE MANAGEMENT WASTE

One of the core ideas of continuous improvement is the elimination of waste. This usually means eliminating unnecessary tasks, motions, inventory, rework, etc. However, the new challenge for lean management is to improve the efficiency of management itself. Much management activity is waste. This waste is just as destructive, or more so, than waste among front line employees.

What does this waste look like? I have identified six forms of management waste. Feel free to add to the list.

Management Waste # 1: Sucking decisions up due to the lack of empowerment, education and encouragement at lower levels. Management thinks they are busy because they are doing other people's work and they do this because they have not structured the organization, established the training and systems to create competent problem-solving and decisions at lower levels.

Management Waste #2: Displaying contradictory models. If you want to teach your children not to smoke, drink or swear, but you walk around the house smoking, drinking and swearing, your efforts are going to be little more than waste. Management, leaders, must model the behavior they desire of others. The failure to do so cripples any change effort. Millions of dollars in consulting and training have become waste because management didn't walk the talk.

Management Waste #3: Failure to define and manage your own processes. There are processes that are owned by the senior management team. Every team, at every level, should have a SIPOC that defines input, output, and value adding processes owned by that team. They don't own any process? Than the entire team is waste! Tell them to go home. MOST management teams do not know what there processes are, and reinvent them in a random or annual manner. Developing strategy is a senior management value-adding process. Where is the map that visualizes how they develop strategy? When they did it last year, did they study the process and what did they learn? Unfortunately, they probably learned nothing and are not themselves engaged in continuous improvement. Therefore, they don't understand it and do not set the model.

Management Waste #4: Failure of decision-making: I have coached dozens of senior management teams. One would think, logically, that the higher you go in the company, the more skilled would be the decision makers and decision-making process. The value of decisions made at the top, should be of greatest value. Errors made at the top are the most expensive. The truth is that in most companies, the decision-making process at the top is terrible.

Many years ago I was doing a socio-tech redesign of a major financial organization on Wall Street. The only room the design team could find to meet in was THE BOARD ROOM!! Very expensive furniture, huge table, mahogany paneled walls, etc. After a day or two the design team had half the wall area covered with flip chart sheets. In stormed the official keeper of the room with steam spurting out of his ears. He yelled, "Take that down immediately! No one has ever put anything on these walls!" I asked, "Really? No one has ever brainstormed or put flip charts on the walls in here?" "Absolutely Not!" He yelled back. Poor fellow. He had never seen a room in which people were actually solving problems, brainstorming, reaching consensus, developing action plans, etc. It tells you a lot about how senior management teams fail to employ disciplined decision processes.

Management Waste #5: Wasted space and resources. That board room was used once a quarter. It sat empty and unused most of the time. Why do managers need larger offices as they move up the ladder. Do they get fatter? Do they have bigger computers or more books? What is that about? It is about waste. It is the waste of ego. The time spent at resorts doing annual strategic planning that could be done in their own conference room, or in someone's home, is also waste. Apply the same disciplined standards of waste and resource utilization at the executive and management level as you apply to the factory floor.

Management Waste #6: The failure of trust. An effective management team, like any team, is a social system built on trust. That trust enables members to share, to ask questions, to offer suggestions, and to listen well to each other. On MOST management teams there is a failure of trust among its members that inhibits their ability to solve problems and make effective decisions.

The solution to these forms of waste, which is the opposite of lean management, is not only training, but coaching and feedback. They need hands on help in order to change their behavior, their habits. It is these habits that define the culture.

Waste Elimination Worksheet

Process:

Steps	Time for Step	Value adding time	%

Improvement Worksheet

Process:

Improvements to Steps: (Inventory, Motion, Transportation, Defects, Waiting Time, Overproduction, Processing)	New Time for Step	Value adding time	%

PART THREE
IMPROVING TEAMWORK

CHAPTER 16

LEADING EFFECTIVE MEETINGS

The success of any team is in large part a function of the process by which it makes decisions, solves problems, and the degree to which members communicate well with each other. This requires effective facilitation. The purpose of this chapter is to present the basic skills of facilitation. The next chapter on listening skills will enhance facilitation and teamwork by all members.

OBJECTIVES:

1. To introduce the basic skills of facilitation.

2. To gain understanding of how all team members can contribute to facilitation.

As you implement lean management an important factor will be developing effective meetings. These meetings may be face-to-face and at other times will be telephone conferences. Some will be quick morning huddles to plan the work for the day, and some will be more in depth problem-solving or planning sessions. But, no matter what the purpose or format, meetings may be efficient or inefficient. We have all been in meetings that were chaotic and frustrating. The goal of this chapter is to make sure that your meetings are productive and enjoyable.

THE SKILLS OF FACILITATING

To facilitate is to make easier for others. We will provide the best possible product or service to our customers if we make things easier for each other. We have to help facilitate each other's work. In meetings we all have to help each other voice our opinions, think together in constructive ways, and reach decisions that will be helpful to all.

It may be useful to first clarify what the facilitator is not. The facilitator is not the person in charge. She is not the boss, the manager, or the formal leader of the group. It may be in some meetings that the manager of the group also serves as the facilitator. However, these are entirely different functions. The formal manager might also serve as the scribe or the timekeeper, but this has nothing to do with her being the formal manager of the group.

The following are the basic skills, the behavior that a facilitator employs to assist the individuals and the group in their effort to make decisions or solve problems.

1. ORGANIZING:

All groups want both order and the opportunity for participation. The first type of order that a facilitator brings to a group is to create and gain agreement to an agenda. Where are we beginning and where are we trying to go, and where are we in the journey? These are the questions that all members want to know, and it is the job of the facilitator to be sure that the journey is clear. But the agenda is only the plan. Keeping the group on the agenda with simple questions like "does that address our topic?" reminds the group what we are trying to accomplish. These are the simple acts of facilitation that a group will find helpful.

2. ESTABLISH THE TOPIC

No one comes to meetings to be entertained. Most people are busy and want to know that their time will be well used. Tell them why you are here. Make it important. If the facilitator doesn't feel that it is important, he or she will never convince the members of the group that it is important. Why am I spending my valuable time here? What difference will this make? Give them a good reason to spend their valuable time. Give them purpose.

Tips for Clarifying the Topic

- State the Topic and Gain Commitment: The facilitator should clearly state what he or she believes to be the topic, look around at the members of the group and ask them if this is their understanding. The act of asking for their commitment will help them to stick to the topic during conversation.

- Write the Topic on a Flip Chart or Have a Printed Agenda: The ability to see, in writing, a topic or decision helps the group members focus, understand, and create unity of thought and action.

- Discuss Outcomes: At the beginning of a meeting it is helpful to both state the purpose and discuss possible outcomes, actions, next steps that might follow the meeting.

3. CLARIFYING:

Very often we are not clear in our communications. Many of those who participate on teams are not entirely comfortable expressing their ideas or feelings to the group. This is particularly true when the topic is one that involves emotions on the part of that member.

A key job of the facilitator is to clarify where we are in the discussion. "Have we identified the facts that matter in this case?" "Have we discussed the causes of a problem?" "Are we in agreement?" "Are we ready to move on to solutions?" "Have we now all agreed on a solution?" "It sounds like we have agreement." Each of these questions or statements helps to clarify where we are in the process of getting to a decision.

4. REFLECTING:

Reflecting is to put the conversation in perspective. "Let me share where I think we are in this conversation. It feels to me that everyone has voiced their opinion, and I think there are basically two approaches being discussed...." This is a statement that reflects on where we are and it is very helpful to the group by giving them a view of where we are on our journey. This then makes clear where we need to go from here. This reflection will also give them an opportunity to share their understanding of where we are in the process. This may be different than yours.

5. MOTIVATING:

Both individuals and groups need encouragement. It is important that the facilitator be someone with an essentially positive outlook, someone who recognizes the progress, the contributions and the hopes about the outcome of our journey. Motivation is infectious, as is discouragement.

Simple things make good facilitation. Saying "Thank you" after someone has made a contribution, particularly if it was difficult for that person, can be very helpful. Nodding your head forward and back, signaling that you understand what the person is saying, is encouraging. Smiling can be a sign of encouragement. Just saying, "good" after someone has spoken is the simplest form of recognition, and it can help motivate members to contribute.

Sometimes the group needs more serious motivation. The group may be stuck on a very difficult point, and it may be helpful for the facilitator to reflect on the group's progress and point out the things they have accomplished, the progress they have made, and then assure them that they will overcome this obstacle as well.

Another aspect of motivation is having fun. Every group should laugh, take time to do things, go somewhere together, and tell jokes, just for the sake of having fun. Teams at work, just like families who have fun together, are more likely to solve problems and trust each other. Having fun is not trivial. It is an important part of what leads to the effectiveness of a team. The facilitator should be thinking about each of these aspects of motivation and thinking about how he can contribute to the motivation of each member of the team.

6. COMFORTING:

If you have spent a lot of time in group meetings, you are probably comfortable making contributions. However, many teams at work are comprised of individuals who are not experienced. The lack of experience leads to discomfort or anxiety. Difficult topics, topics concerning the behavior of members of the group, or issues that may threaten our position in the group or in our job rightfully cause us anxiety.

What does a facilitator do to help create comfort in a group when some members have these anxieties? One important skill of a facilitator is to express empathy. Empathy statements usually begin with the following:

"I can understand that... (the reason for their concern)....may cause you to feel (a word like 'worried', or 'upset')."

"It sounds like you feel...(a feeling word like 'upset')...because...(the reason)."

"It must be ... (feeling work like "difficult, or painful")...when ... (the circumstance causing the difficulty).

7. RESOLVING CONFLICTS:

In almost any group there will be times when conflicts arise among members of the group. These conflicts can be simple matters of disagreement on a topic, or they can be more severe conflicts between two people who don't trust each other, or one may have been offended by the other.

Your best tools to resolve conflicts are your listening skills that are discussed in the next chapter. Your ability to demonstrate genuine understanding of the position and feelings of both parties helps to reduce their frustration or anger.

There is another critical skill in resolving conflicts and that is the thought process of looking for points of unity. When two people are in conflict, for example, over a course of action to solve a problem, it is helpful to point to their agreement, or point of unity. For example you might say "It's great that you are both concerned about solving this problem." Or, you can look for the elements of their solutions that are in agreement – "It sounds like you both agree that this is a priority and you also both feel that we should ..." (then add the parts of the solution on which they agree).

It is then helpful to clarify the points of disagreement in a clear and objective way. That objectivity may have been lost in their passion to express their views. It may be helpful then to turn to other members of the group and ask them to identify the pros and cons of each alternative.

Here are a few things you may do to create unity from differences.

RECOGNIZE THE VALIDITY OF EXPERIENCE

It may be easy to facilitate a group of ten white male accountants who graduated from the same school, have been through the same training courses, and work for the same company. Of course, they are likely to think in very similar ways. But we often have team members with totally different backgrounds and experiences, and they may arrive at different understandings of the same events.

As a facilitator it is helpful to think that everyone is "right" from his or her point of view. Based on their experience, as they understand the issue, given the facts they know, what they say is right to them. The difficulty is that no one else has the exact same experience. Many disagreements are simply based on the different "data" that we each possess. The facilitator can simply ask, "There are two very different views here. What do you think might be the different experiences that result in these different views?" Asking the question in this manner transforms the issue from who is right or wrong to how and why diverse backgrounds result in diverse views.

IT IS NOT ALWAYS EITHER-OR

A facilitator was assisting the Board of Directors and the staff of a school to develop their vision and strategic plan. There had been a history of tension at the school between those who felt that the most important thing was for children to enjoy learning, to develop love of learning, and those who felt it was important to develop competence, knowledge of reading, writing, and arithmetic. The conflict was categorized as the liberals versus the conservatives, the soft approach versus the hard approach.

The facilitator could see the participants in the room lining up behind each of these views' arguments. It appeared that there was a fundamental difference in what was viewed as important in education.

The facilitator, seeking to resolve this conflict, drew this matrix on a flip chart and explained that there are two dimensions being discussed, and they are both good and important. But are they necessarily contrary? Isn't it possible to do a great job of imparting knowledge and, at the same time, do a great job of causing children to love the process of learning? He also asked those who thought knowledge was most important how parents viewed the school. They felt the school was high on creating love, and low on creating knowledge. In other words, the knowledge people thought the school was North-West on the matrix. He then asked the love of learning group how they viewed the school today. They viewed it has being South-East, low on love and high on knowledge.

You can image how the poor staff felt. Bombarded and not appreciated by either group. The staff felt the school was in the North-East quadrant. After much discussion they all agreed that what was important was for the school to be North-East. Neither group felt the other group's concern was unimportant. They both wanted the same thing.

This is an example of how a matrix, a simple tool for looking at two different qualities at the same time, can help resolve conflicts and create unity.

OK, WE SEE IT DIFFERENTLY

Finally, the facilitator may not be able to reconcile two different points of view. It may be useful to simply acknowledge the differences and accept them.

I like blue and you like red. Do we have to resolve that? There are many different points of view, preferences, and interpretations of events that do not need to be resolved. They need to be left behind.

When resolving conflicts between two members of the team try the following:

- ✓ Clarify the points on which the parties agree.

- ✓ Clarify the disagreement and the reason for that disagreement. Check this out with them.

- ✓ Express empathy or understanding of both of their views so that they feel "heard."

- ✓ Ask the rest of the group if they have other alternatives, or ask them to discuss the pros and cons of the different solutions.

✓ Ask the group for criteria, what is important, in solving this problem.

✓ Ask the group if there is a way to take the best parts of each solution and combine them.

✓ Ask the group if there is then a consensus point of view, or ask the group to vote on a solution.

8. CONTROLLING – PLAYING "COP":

Every group gets "out-of-control" from time to time. In fact, it is a sign of a healthy comfort level that the group will drift into social periods where members are talking about their children or the weekend baseball came and be "off-task." This is when the facilitator, perhaps after letting the group enjoy some "play-time," will have to get the group back "on-task."

It is important to do this in a way that is not punitive or bossy. Some facilitators have a little bell they ring, or tapping on a glass or cup, can get everyone's attention and you can just say "Let's get back on-task, folks!" or, "Time-out, we need to go back to work!" Or, you may need to remind the group of their time constraints, which there always are.

A good facilitator has a comfortable sense of how and when to exert control. It is important that the group doesn't come to feel that the facilitator is excessively controlling or they may rebel. A good facilitator knows how much "play-time" to allow the group before calling for control.

EXERCISE:

Consider a meeting you have attended that was both highly productive and which had a spirit of unity. How did the facilitator behave that encouraged this environment? How did other members behave to help create this environment? What did the facilitator do to make all feel welcome?

_____

_____

_____

Recall a meeting that was tense, anxiety provoking, and lacking unity and harmony. Again, how did the facilitator or other members of the group behave that resulted in this feeling?

_____

_____

_____

When considering these two meetings, what are the implications for facilitation skills? How did listening contribute to these conditions? How could effective listening have improved these meetings?

_____

_____

GROUP PROCESS SELF-ASSESSMENT

This is an assessment to identify how you can improve your group problem-solving and decision-making. This may be used by any group that has responsibility for making team decisions and implementing those decisions. It should not be used to judge that we are "good" or "bad" or to criticize. Rather, it is to be used to say "exactly what is it that we can improve?" and, "are we doing better now than before?"

This self-assessment should be scored by all the members of the team, the scores added up, and then you can ask a) "which items do we feel good about?" and, b) "which items do we most need to improve?" Identify specific actions you can take to improve and then review the progress on those at future meetings.

On each of the following items indicate the degree to which you agree with the statement.

		Disagree		Somewhat Agree		Agree
1.	My group has a clear purpose that all the members understand.	0	2.5	5	7.5	10
2.	My group meets at a regular time and location.	0	2.5	5	7.5	10
3.	The location where we meet is free of distractions and is comfortable.	0	2.5	5	7.5	10
4.	We have flip chart or white board to use in problem-solving and decision-making.	0	2.5	5	7.5	10
5.	We prepare ourselves before the meeting by reviewing information that has been distributed.	0	2.5	5	7.5	10
6.	When we meet the topic is clarified by the chairperson/facilitator.	0	2.5	5	7.5	10
7.	The members are good at staying focused on the topic.	0	2.5	5	7.5	10
8.	The chairperson/facilitator provides the opportunity for all to participate.	0	2.5	5	7.5	10
9.	The members of the group are sensitive to, and respectful of, cultural differences and styles of participation.	0	2.5	5	7.5	10
10.	When we consult on an issue we discuss the principles that underlie or are important to this issue.	0	2.5	5	7.5	10
11.	Before suggesting possible solutions, we gather and examine the facts pertaining to this issue.	0	2.5	5	7.5	10
12.	When discussing possible solutions or courses of action we allow time for brainstorming, free thinking without judgment, to allow for creative ideas.	0	2.5	5	7.5	10
13.	We use a flip chart or white board so everyone can see and reflect on previous	0	2.5	5	7.5	10

		Disagree	Somewhat Agree			Agree
	ideas, helping to create unity of thought.					
14.	When new ideas are presented the members consider the ideas without prejudice (who they come from) or bias (holding to previous ideas).	0	2.5	5	7.5	10
15.	When discussing problems we tend not to blame individuals, but study and improve the process.	0	2.5	5	7.5	10
16.	We reach consensus by considering all the ideas that have been presented, considering their pros and cons, and narrowing them to a critical few.	0	2.5	5	7.5	10
17.	When we reach a decision the chairperson or facilitator clarifies the decision and gains commitment from all members of the group.	0	2.5	5	7.5	10
18.	Decisions are written down so all can see and review the decision.	0	2.5	5	7.5	10
19.	Each decision is followed by an Action Plan, which specifies *Who* will do *What* by *When*.	0	2.5	5	7.5	10
20.	At each meeting, the prior action plans are reviewed and revised as needed.	0	2.5	5	7.5	10

CHAPTER 17

EFFECTIVE LISTENING SKILLS

The ability to listen well to others, to not only hear, but to understand, is an essential skill for all team members. This chapter is intended both to present the skills of effective listening and to practice those skills within the team.

OBJECTIVES:

1. To gain understanding of the critical skills of listening to others.

2. To practice and develop this skill.

Effective listening skills are the most essential skills of a good facilitator. Listening does not mean simply not talking and waiting for the other person to finish. Listening is the process of gaining understanding, checking your understanding with the other person, and encouraging the other person to express herself fully and frankly. Effective listening skills are also the most important skills in the process of creating unity within a group. If we truly listen to each other, rather than quickly reacting to what we think the other person said, we will cause unity and harmony to be achieved.

Effective listening skills are comprised of five component skills. These are *asking questions*, *expressing empathy*, *rephrasing*, *acknowledging*, and the use of *silence*. We will consider and practice each of these. They are also important skills in one-to-one communication in the family, at work, or in any other setting. Without a doubt, the best communicators are the best listeners. The worst communicators talk endlessly.

Please take note that these skills are not ONLY for the formal facilitator. Every member of the team has a responsibility to help facilitate, to help make it easier for other members to give their best contribution to the team.

A. ASKING OPEN-ENDED QUESTIONS

The act of asking questions demonstrates interest in the other person, opens the opportunity for the other person to voice their views and feelings, and leads to understanding. Facilitating a team is one part speaking and ten parts asking questions and listening.

Different types of questions lead to different results. The skilled listener knows when to use different types of questions. There are two types of questions: open-ended and closed-ended questions.

Imagine that you are meeting with your team members. You can see that one of your associates is just staring off into the distance. You can see that her eyes are beginning to tear and her head turns down avoiding the gaze of others.

In a quivering voice she says "This is very hard for me. I'm not sure I can do this." Everyone is silent as they wait for her to continue.

"It happened last night" she continues in sobbing voice. "I had just arrived home from work. I didn't think I had done anything wrong. I can't image what I did to cause this. I was totally unprepared for this." Again she looks down and is overcome by sobbing. It is almost too difficult for her to continue.

You start to imagine what horrible thing must have happened. You say to her, "Take your time, Jane. We will do whatever we can to be helpful." She still seems too grieved to continue.

Harold, one of the team members asks, "Jane, does this have to do with your children? Is there a problem with one of your dear children?"

Jane looks up, appearing somewhat surprised and says "Oh, no, my children are fine."

Another team member, Bob, then asks, "Jane is there a problem between you and your husband. Maybe we can help you. You know several of us have faced our own marriage issues. I know your husband and he is a good person even if he does have some faults."

Jane looks up again and looks somewhat puzzled. Jane says, "I don't think there is a problem with my husband. Actually, I am sorry to say, but, it's my dog. He died last night?"

The members of the group then look at each other surprised and embarrassed. Jane then looks at Bob and asks, "What faults do you think my husband has?"

What could have been done by members of the group to handle this situation better?

_____

_____

_____

The key in this situation is in the types of questions that were asked. "Is there something wrong with your children?" is a closed-ended question. It can be answered with a "yes" or "no." Any question that can be answered "yes" or "no" is a closed-ended question. It is, essentially, a guess. "Is there a problem with one of your children" is a closed-ended question. You can guess a lot of things before asking the right closed-ended question. And, as you can see, some of those guesses could get you in trouble.

Closed-ended questions do not elicit conversation from the other person. In this case, they did not elicit Jane's own ideas or feelings. If you ask a series of closed-ended questions, it feels like you are playing Twenty-Questions, trying to guess the right question. In the scene described above, how many questions of this type would the group members have had to ask to finally arrive at the question "Did your dog die?" - Probably hundreds!

An open-ended question usually begins with what, where, why or how.

- *How can we help you?*

- *What seems to be the problem?*

- *What happened last night?*

- *Why are you upset?*

- *Where were you when you first felt this way?*

These are all open-ended questions. Notice that none of them can be answered with a "yes" or "no." You can see why all good conversationalists have the habit of asking open-ended questions.

How you ask questions is often a matter of habit. To develop the habit of asking open-ended questions, let's practice. First, here are several statements that might be made in a meeting. Don't respond with a statement or argument. Respond with a question. Write down several open-ended questions that you might use in response to these statements:

"I am so tired of those customers changing their schedules. Don't they realize how difficult it makes my life?"

_____

_____

_____

"These meetings are a waste of time! We never decide anything. Why doesn't management just tell us what to do and let us do our work?"

_____

_____

_____

"I am doing my job. I just wish everyone else on this team would do their job. Then I wouldn't have to waste my time listening to y'all just yap about this being wrong and that being wrong!"

_____

_____

_____

Open-ended questions can be useful in a number of situations:

- ✓ To Start A Discussion: "What do you think about the new marketing plan?" Or, "How did you feel about our performance?"

- ✓ To Include A Member of the Group: "John, how do you feel about this issue?" "Serena, what is your experience on this issue?"

- ✓ To Bring a Conversation Back to Topic: "What other information do we need to make this decision?" Or, "On the subject of how we should plan this project, what other steps should we take?"

- ✓ To Make a Transition from One Agenda Item to the Next: "Before we summarize our decision, what other thoughts do you have on this subject?"

EXERCISE:

Now form groups of three. Have one member present a problem or concern related to your work. This can be entirely fictitious or real. State this problem in one brief sentence. A second member of the group now asks at least three open-ended questions that cause the first person to reveal more about the concern. The third person will serve as a coach and give the person asking the questions feedback or help if they get stuck. Rotate roles until each person has practiced each role.

How did it feel to be asked these open-ended questions? How would it have felt if the questions were closed-ended? Did you find that asking these types of questions was natural or difficult?

_____

_____

_____

B. Expressing Empathy

An empathy statement expresses how you think the other person feels and why. Showing empathy towards another person helps that person feel like a part of the group, is a cause of unity between the group members, and reduces any tendency to respond negatively or defensively. We all have a strong need to know that our feelings are understood.

It takes courage to express personal feelings in a group. Those feelings are often an important component of group problem-solving. Problem-solving that includes all of the facts, but none of the feelings, is not likely to lead to unified action.

Here are some models for empathy statements:

"It sounds as if you feel... (..add in a feeling word) ... because... (reason)."

For example: "It sounds as if you feel upset that we don't have the resources for this project because everyone is too busy."

Or, "It sounds as if you feel anxious because you have to make that presentation tomorrow."

"It must be...(feeling word)...*when*...(reason)."

For example: "It must be frustrating to work so hard on a project when no one else appears to recognize that work."

Or, "It must be annoying when it seems that no one is listening to your point of view."

"I can understand that...(reason)...*would make you*...(feeling word)."

For example: "I can understand that the amount of time it took us to make a decision would make you upset."

Or, "I can understand that getting appointed to this new job would be very exciting for you."

Each of these statements demonstrates that you are at least attempting to understand how the other person feels. These empathy statements can defuse emotions that might get in the way of progress, and they can allow the other person to clarify her own feelings if your understanding is not exactly correct. These are all helpful outcomes.

A facilitator may use empathy statements...

✓ To help reduce strong emotions that may prevent rational thinking and conversation. Making an empathy statement to someone who is expressing pain or anger can diffuse those feelings. Empathy is like someone holding your hand, letting you know that they understand. For example, "I can see that you are really hurt that you were embarrassed in front of your friends."

✓ To encourage other people to listen. If others feel that you are genuinely recognizing the emotions of a member of the group, they. will recognize this model, and they are more likely to feel empathy and listen to the other person.

✓ To relieve anxiety about discussing a problem publicly. In a team setting it is difficult for many people to express their own feelings. Many of us are "private people." A statement such as "I can understand that you are concerned about...." relieves some of the anxiety and makes communication easier.

EXERCISE:

Form small groups and practice making empathy statements. One person should present a situation that caused some emotion and the other person should listen, and then express empathy with the other person, using one of the models above. Switch roles until each person has an opportunity to practice expressing empathy.

How did you feel when the listener expressed empathy for your situation?

_____

_____

_____

How did you feel expressing empathy for others?

_____

_____

_____

C. Rephrasing or Reflective Listening

Rephrasing, or reflective listening, is a way of checking out your understanding of what you think the other person meant to say. Conveying emotions or deep thoughts on any matter is a difficult thing. When we speak, we make an effort to convey our *meaning*, our intended thought or feeling. However, what we *meant* and what the other person *receives* or understands are often not the same thing.

For example, during a meeting of nurses responsible for health and safety a member says, "I've had it! I just can't do this anymore. I am tired of trying to get people to wash their hands."

Another member then says, "So, I hear you saying you don't want to be on the health and safety committee anymore."

"No, no, no! I mean I am tired of having to remind these people, saying the same thing over and over again. There's never any consequence to them."

You can see that her first communication in which she says "I just can't do this anymore!" she is expressing an emotion, and the words can be interpreted in several different ways. If the listener assumed that he knew what she meant by those words, rather than checking out what he heard, there would have been a misunderstanding.

Often, when we hear someone express a thought or emotion our impulse is to respond, react, answer or even argue. We want to act on what we think we hear. In doing so we often create more of a problem because we are reacting to what we think we hear, not what the other person intends to communicate. In this manner two people can be talking right past each other.

Let's replay the conversation above.

She says, "I've had it! I just can't do this anymore. I am tired of trying to get people to wash their hands."

Another member says, "Well, you can quit if you want, but I was appointed to this committee and its part of my job and I'm doing my job whether you do or not!"

"Oh, please!" she responds, "stop playing holier than thou."

"Excuse me. But I don't think doing your duty should be taken lightly."

What just happened here?

Did this create more understanding or misunderstanding? Was the cause of unity served or was disunity created?

If we react to what we think we heard, we often increase the gap in understanding between us and the other person. With all good intentions, we may create hurt feelings and damage the motivation of the other person. If we check out, reflect, rephrase what we think we heard, and give the other person the opportunity to clarify, we can often create understanding and harmony rather than dissonance.

Rephrasing implies and conveys a sense of humility. It conveys that you are not sure that you understood the other person, and you would like them to clarify so you can improve your understanding. This humility tends to defuse emotions and serves the cause of unity.

Rephrasing statements start with phrases such as:

What I'm hearing is...

So, in other words you (think, feel that)...

So, it sounds as if...

Let me make sure I've got this right, you...

A facilitator may use rephrasing...

- ✓ **To clarify a group member's statements**. "It sounds as if you are ready to move on to the next subject."

- ✓ **To resolve conflicts between two group members.** "I hear you saying that we need to emphasize this at our next meeting, and I heard John say that he also felt this was very important."

- ✓ **To help someone express their emotions.** "What I hear you saying is that you feel very strongly about this and it has caused you considerable pain."

- ✓ **To get at a deeper understanding of the issue than may have been expressed.** "So, it sounds like this is not merely about what time and place we meet, but about what we value, what is most important to us."

EXERCISE:

Try rephrasing each of the following statements in your own words. Use one of the above lead off phrases to express, in your own words, what you think the other person means.

"I think we should ask Mary to lead the effort to deal with the supplier problems because she never stops talking about that!"

_____

_____

_____

"I'm sorry, but I don't care if I am the oldest nurse here, I simply can't stand in front of new employees and teach a class on the history of this hospital! I just can't do that!"

_____

_____

_____

"I am not sure I can keep working here. There have been so many changes and so much uncertainty; it really drives me crazy!"

_____

_____

_____

Share your rephrasing with other members of your group and listen to how they reflected their understanding of these statements. Discuss how you think the speaker would have reacted to each of these different statements. You will probably find that different people heard different meaning in these statements. That's why it's a good idea to reflect and seek clarification.

D. ACKNOWLEDGING

Sometimes an effective listening skill is so simple and subtle that it is easy not to notice. For example, eye contact. If you are talking and the listener's eyes are wandering around the room, it would be easy to feel that he was not really listening. Good listeners acknowledge that they are listening by simply looking at the speaker.

Body language, particularly head movement, may convey that you are listening and have understood the other person. When facilitating a team meeting someone may raise their hand and start asking a question that has a negative tone, as if they feel that you have said something that is not correct. By looking at them and gently nodding your head forward and aft, you are conveying that you hear them and consider the point they are making to have worth. This tends to defuse the situation and makes everyone, including you, more comfortable.

When a member of the group offers an idea or suggestion you may simply say, "right" or "I can understand that" or "good point." These are all simple responses that let the other person know that they have been heard.

E. USING SILENCE

As the facilitator of a group, is it necessary that you respond to every comment made by a member of the group?

No. Sometimes it is best to simply let a comment digest; allow time for quiet reflection or meditation on a comment. You might then ask the group "How do the rest of you feel about that?"

This may be particularly useful if someone has expressed anger or a very negative emotion. Rather than confront, or attempt to empathize, it may work well to simply let the remark sit there for ten, twenty seconds. Then you might say "That's an interesting point of view. It sounds like this has been bothering you for quite a while. Does anyone have any thoughts as to how we might resolve that?"

As a facilitator remember that it is not your responsibility to have an answer or solution to every issue or emotion. It is your responsibility to facilitate learning and to create unity. Sometimes, if you try too hard to resolve every issue, you may find that you are working too hard and actually creating anxiety in the group. And, remember that the entire group has a responsibility to assist in the facilitation and make it easier for all members to contribute.

You can see that the use of each of these listening skills requires practice and good judgment. This comes only with experience and reflection on your own facilitation. Practice using these skills with your customers, your children, your spouse, as well as with team members. They are skills that will serve you well throughout your life.

CHAPTER 18

STRAIGHT-TALK
GIVING AND RECEIVING FEEDBACK

The purpose of this chapter is to develop the skills of effectively giving feedback to others and receiving feedback in a way that leads to learning and improvement.

OBJECTIVES:

1. To learn and to practice giving feedback to others in a manner that will facilitate learning by the other person.

2. To learn and practice the skill of receiving feedback in a manner that will improve your own ability to learn from others.

Many team members have developed a habit of getting along, keeping quiet and not causing trouble. They survive. But, do they learn, do they engage in continuous improvement?

What happens when members of a team fail to use straight-talk, fail to express how they really think or feel about a matter? Group-think is a failure of teams to speak up, honestly, or express how they really feel. The ability to give straight-talk, to give and to receive feedback from others, is essential to well-functioning teams.

THE ROAD TO ABILENE

Jerry Harvey, in The Abilene Paradox[18], tells a wonderful story about his family, when he was young, sitting on the porch one evening in the sweltering heat of west Texas and someone asks "What's for dinner?" Someone then mentions a restaurant down the road in Abilene. Somehow they end up in the car, with no air conditioning, the dust blowing through the windows and everyone miserable, when Ma asks Pa, "Why the hell are you dragging us to Abilene anyway?" To which Pa says, "I ain't draggin' you anywhere, you wanted to go to Abilene." "Did not" replies Ma. And the question comes, how did they end up on the road to Abilene when no one wanted to go in the first place?

As Jerry Harvey, a college professor, tells it, he was sitting in his office one day when an attractive young woman student came into his office sat down and looked rather depressed. Dr. Harvey, concerned, asked "What's wrong, you look rather depressed?" And, she replied, "Well, you'd be depressed too if next weekend you were marrying someone you didn't love." To which he naturally responded, "Well, why are you marrying someone you don't love." And she explained, "Well it was a moment of passion, and I couldn't say no; it would have broken his heart. And, he told his folks, and they called mine, and the wedding got planned, and I can't say no now. I just couldn't do that to him."

The next day Dr. Harvey was sitting in his office and a young man came in and sat down, looking rather depressed. The ever-empathetic Dr. Harvey asked, "What's wrong, you look rather depressed?" And, he replied, "Well, you'd be depressed too if next weekend you were marrying someone you didn't love." To which he naturally responded, "Well, why are you marrying someone you don't love?" And he explained, "Well it was a moment of passion, and I couldn't say no, I would have

---

[18] Harvey, Jerry. *The Abilene Paradox and Other Meditations on Management.* Jossey-Bass Inc., Publishers, San Francisco, 1996.

broken her heart. And, she told her folks, and they called mine, and the wedding got planned, and I can't say no now; I just couldn't do that to her."

Witness a young couple "on the road to Abilene." How does a group get on the road to Abilene? It is a simple matter of assuming someone else knows the answers or just failing to express your true feelings and opinions. It is often because the great "why" question isn't asked by anyone. It is a failure of honest inquiry. This is how major corporations, even entire industries, ended up in Abilene. And, it happens to teams every day.

EXERCISE:

Has your team or organization ever been on the "road to Abilene?" Have you seen any other group of people going down this road? Describe how you think this happened?

_____

_____

_____

_____

What are the exact behaviors or lack of behavior that result in a group going down this road?

_____

_____

_____

GIVING AND RECEIVING FEEDBACK

One of the most common reasons for poor performance and problems among team members is that members of the group fail to give each other honest feedback, what some call *straight talk*.

Why do we hold things inside and fail to share them with our team? We may say the following things to ourselves:

- "If I am the only one who feels this way, it must just be me."
- "If I raise this subject, it will start an argument, and I don't want to argue."
- "If I really say how I feel, I will hurt his feelings and make matters worse."

Each of these thoughts is a prescription for getting "on the road to Abilene." It is important that we know when to give feedback. There is no rule, but there are some thoughts that may be helpful.

- First, is the feedback I have to give intended to be genuinely helpful to the other person or group?
- Can I express it in a way that will point to positive action, rather than only expressing anger?
- Can I give the feedback in a way that does not demean the person, but rather focuses on specific behavior?

If your answer to these questions is yes, you should probably give the person or group the feedback you have.

GUIDELINES FOR GIVING FEEDBACK

The following guidelines may be helpful when considering how to give another person, or the team, feedback.

1. Be sure that your intention is to be helpful to the other person or team.
2. Think it through. Be clear about what you want to say. Even if you are not sure about the reasons why you feel the way you do, you can share that uncertainty.
3. Emphasize the positive. You care about this person or group and you want to help them improve. Tell them why you care.
4. Be specific -- Avoid general comments or exaggerations. Don't say "You always..." This will cause the other person to be defensive. Be specific about what and when the person or group does something.
5. Focus on pinpointed behavior rather than the person. The person is good and worthy (why you care) but the behavior is what is bothering you, and it is also what the person can change.
6. Own the feedback -- Use 'I' statements to indicate that this is how "I feel and others may not experience the same thing."

7. Your manner and the feelings you express are important. Be direct, but be kind and helpful. Be sincere.

GUIDELINES FOR RECEIVING FEEDBACK

We can all benefit from feedback... IF we listen well and seek to understand in a way that will promote our own learning and development. Here are some guidelines for receiving feedback from others:

1. Understand that the person giving you feedback is attempting to be helpful. Try to receive the feedback as a gift given to you by this person who wishes to help you succeed.
2. Listen for actionable feedback. Ask yourself "What can I do differently in the future based on this feedback?" Do not focus on the person giving you the feedback or how you feel about that individual.
3. Ask for clarification. Ask when or under what circumstances you do something. Ask for examples that can clarify the situation or behavior. Ask the other person what you might do as an alternative in that situation. Seek to understand.
4. Engage in problem-solving. Think together about the problem.
5. Summarize what you have heard. Reflect back to the person giving you feedback your understanding of what you have heard.
6. Take responsibility for your behavior and demonstrate a willingness to modify your own behavior.
7. Remember that this feedback is not an evaluation of how good a person you are, but how your behavior is perceived by others at certain times.

A MODEL FOR GIVING FEEDBACK

This simple model may be helpful when giving another person or a group feedback:

- **Ask permission** ("I would like to share a feeling I have, if you don't mind."
- **When...** (Describe the circumstance, time, etc.)
- **What happens** (describe the specific behavior)
- **It makes me feel...** (why it is a problem for me and possibly for others)

- **A suggestion.** It is always best not to act as if you know for certain what the right course of action is, but it is helpful to have a possible or suggested course of action.

For example: "If you don't mind, I would like to share a concern I have. *(Permission)* When we get on a topic that everyone is interested in *(When)* we lose track of the time and our meetings go ten or fifteen minutes over time. *(What happens?)* I have children that I need to pick up after our meetings and this makes me very anxious I am going to be late. *(How it makes me feel)* Could we have a timekeeper give us a ten minute warning, then a five minute warning, before our meeting are supposed to end?" *(Suggestion)*

The following are exercises and experiences that you may find helpful to improve the team dynamics in each of the five categories.

TEAM FEEDBACK EXERCISE

It will be helpful to practice using this model. Practice giving feedback to the entire team. The purpose of this exercise is to give every member of the team the opportunity to give the entire team some feedback that may be on their mind.

- The facilitator should instruct the team that the feedback they are going to give is for the entire team, not directed at any one person.
- Give the group fifteen minutes to write down the feedback they have using the model and guidelines described above.
- When the group is ready, tell them that we are going to go around the room and everyone will have a chance to give their feedback, but we are NOT going to stop to react or analyze each statement.
- After everyone has made their statement, ask the group the following questions:
  - o What was most helpful in terms of how these statements were made?
  - o What feelings did you have and what caused these feelings?
  - o If we were just receiving any one of these at a time, how would we respond?
  - o What does this experience tell us about what our team should do in the future?

ONE-TO-ONE FEEDBACK EXERCISE

The purpose of this exercise is to practice giving and receiving feedback between team members.

Directions:

- The first stage of this exercise is to practice the skill of observing behavior. On the following page you will find a "Behavior Observation" sheet. You will ask each member of the team to use this sheet to observe behaviors that are both helpful and not helpful to the progress of the team.
- Pair up the team members so each member is paired with another.
- Ask every member of the team to observe the behavior of their partner over the next two team meetings. Ask them to observe both desirable and undesirable behavior and indicate the affect those behaviors have on other team members.
- At the third meeting of the team have the group break down into their pairs. Each partner should be in a chair directly facing the other.
- Review the guidelines for both giving and receiving feedback, above. Also review the model for giving feedback. Ask them to spend ten minutes planning how they will give the other feedback using the model and following the guidelines.
- Then ask them to share the feedback with each other, giving time for each of them to both give and receive feedback. This will take approximately fifteen minutes.
- Then ask them to share with each other how they felt receiving the feedback and share suggestions for how both giving and receiving feedback might be improved.

Debrief:

With the group back together, ask the following questions:

- What did you learn from this experience in terms of the process of giving and receiving feedback?
- If you were to give an employee feedback outside of the team, would this impact how you would do that?

- Do you think practicing giving and receiving feedback will increase or decrease your comfort in doing this in the future?
- What are the implications for how we work together as a team?

CHAPTER 19

DIALOGUE: THINKING TOGETHER RATHER THAN ALONE

The quality of conversations within the team will determine the success of problem-solving and collaboration. It will also contribute to the bonds and unity between team members. The purpose of this chapter is to help the team examine those conversations and strive to move from a culture of debate to one of dialogue.

OBJECTIVES

1. To assess the quality of conversation within the team.

2. To create awareness of the cultural patterns of discussion that are normal within the team and which may hinder the team's ability to solve problems.

3. To provide the key skills of dialogue to enhance the quality of conversation and increase the ability of the team to solve problems and to achieve unity of understanding and action.

All conversations are not equal. Have you ever sat down to talk with someone, perhaps someone who you never met before, and felt that they were completely understanding, completely aware of what you were saying, how you were feeling and the meaning behind your words? Do you remember how that made you feel to be so well understood?

Have you ever sat down and talked with someone and felt, no matter how hard you tried, that they just didn't get it? They just could not understand, or worse, seemed to misunderstand everything you said. Even worse, have you had the experience of speaking to someone and they just seemed to want to disagree with everything you said, no matter how simple and true your statements? Do you remember how you became frustrated, and perhaps argumentative in response?

The nature of conversation is, largely determined by culture. We learn to talk to each other in ways that become comfortable and acceptable to us. Native Americans may sit and talk with each other in very quiet voices and almost never look each other in the eye, a gesture they regard as a sign of disrespect. A group of old Jewish men in New York may sit on a park bench and to a stranger passing by, may appear angry and agitate, but in their minds are simply passing the day in friendly conversation. Native islanders in the South Pacific may sit in complete silence for a long time, thinking and then speaking only after they have thought about a matter in great depth. These cultural speech patterns are neither right nor wrong. They each represent a language of communication. But a team in the workplace is usually comprised of individuals with different cultural patterns as well as the personal patterns each member has learned from their family or other experience. These patterns of behavior can help or hinder the decision-making and unity of the group.

THINKING TOGETHER VERSUS THINKING ALONE

One understanding of conversation in a group is to think about the group as a number of different people, individuals with different perspectives or ideas, each member of the group sharing his or her ideas and the group deciding which idea is the best and moving forward with that idea. With this understanding, each individual is thinking alone, forming his or her own ideas and opinions and then attempting to convince the others of the value of those ideas. The "locus" of thought is internal, focused on the self, and "my" ideas, "my" contribution, the acceptance of "my" views over those of another.

Another understanding of group conversation is to consider that the group is thinking as one system, one organism, or one collective mind. With this understanding, the individual members are not so focused on their own ideas or their own opinions. They are less focused on convincing others to accept their ideas. They are not trying to "win". They are just as interested in understanding the ideas of others, trying to find the best solution for the group, regardless of who it comes from. When thinking together, the members are interested in encouraging and supporting the ideas of others because those ideas become their own. The objective is to create "collective wisdom", to find the best answer for the group, with no concern for whose idea it is.

It may be useful to define our terms since we will use these terms as a reference throughout this chapter.

Conversation will be used to describe all interaction among a group of people in their effort to reach a decision or understanding regardless of the quality or nature of that interaction.

Debate is a conversation in which the parties assume opposing positions and view the goal of the conversation to be the victory of their position over that of their opponent.

Discussion is a conversation in which the goal is to reach a decision that both parties can accept and which may represent a compromise or combination of positions previously held by the parties.

Dialogue is a conversation that explores the meaning and nature of an issue in an effort to create insight and understanding on a deeper level. Dialogue seeks to gain the insight of all parties and create collective wisdom, unity, or a new way of looking at an issue.

EXERCISE:

If you had to choose the most common style of conversation in your group, would you describe it as debate, discussion, or dialogue?

_____

_____

How does this style of conversation usually make you feel?

_____

_____

What effect does this style have on your behavior in the group?

_____

_____

Would you want to change this style of conversation? Why?

_____

_____

It may be helpful to visualize how we communicate with others. The following triangle illustrates the mental framework from which we engage in conversation. In most conversations, particularly those conditioned by current culture in Western societies, people are thinking about their own ideas and how to persuade the other person to accept their ideas. Unfortunately, the other person is doing the same. This defeats the opportunity for shared understanding and may result in conflict. When we are in our own corner, thinking alone, we are in a win-lose posture, searching for victory for our position at the cost of defeat for the other person.

Think of the shaded area of the triangle as the locus of thought, where you are thinking, or who is involved in your thinking. At the bottom of the triangle we are in our own corner, thinking alone. The bottom of the triangle represents debate, an all too common mode of discourse in our culture.

When we are trying to win a debate, to have our ideas victorious over the ideas of another, we listen to the other with an ear to exclude and label those ideas in a way that makes them unacceptable.

WHEN TO PRACTICE DIALOGUE, DISCUSSION OR DEBATE

While this chapter presents dialogue as an ideal or desired style of conversation, does that mean that all conversation should be a dialogue? Imagine that you are driving in your car and your children shout "Mom, there's a McDonald's. Can we get a Happy Meal?" Should Mom now enter into a deep and meaningful dialogue about why they really want a Happy Meal, or the true understanding of a Happy Meal? I think not. Mom will probably, and correctly reply, "No, it is almost dinner time and we will be home soon." End of discussion -- and hopefully with no debate.

Our lives are filled with simple decisions, and our concern is often for efficiency and not depth of meaning. In team meetings, much of the time may be reviewing numbers, brainstorming a cause or solution of a specific problem, or deciding who will fill in for someone who will be absent next week These decisions do not require in-depth dialogue.

Dialogue helps us reach consensus decisions. It should be employed for questions of significance. Why are we organized the way we are? Are we genuinely meeting the current and future needs of our customers? Are we assisting each other in the development of our personal capacities? Are we doing the best we can to make this an enjoyable and fulfilling place to work? These are important questions, and they are not matters of just choosing "A" or "B." Rather, they are issues with several levels of meaning and possible action. These are the types of issues around which we should engage in genuine dialogue.

Dialogue can be a frame of reference. Once the team understands the potential of dialogue and its tools, a team member may recognize that we are engaged in a debate when we should be engaged in a dialogue. It is helpful to simply ask "shouldn't we have a dialogue on this issue for a while?" This will trigger a different thought pattern in all the members of the team.

ACHIEVING THE VALUE OF "WE"

The concept of unity was integral to Native American culture, and the symbol of the circle had religious importance as a symbol of the oneness of the human family. When Europeans conquered the continent, they built square houses with square windows cut out, sat around a square, chopped up the land into square acres, and arranged their houses into square blocks. They even did square dancing, which is so unnatural that it requires a supervisor shouting directions to the dancers! A square has four equal sides, and each side has a distinct point of beginning and ending. The sides of a square are connected but individual and separate, four separate lines.

Native Americans tended to live in round tents or huts. They sat in circles when making decisions. They formed their tents into larger circles and danced in circles. Where does a circle begin or end? It can begin anywhere or end nowhere. It is one, a complete unity. Is this merely an interesting coincidence of symbols? Or does the square and circle represent some pattern of thought and behavior? Europeans were certainly better at engineering bridges and mechanical objects. But, perhaps Native Americans were better at understanding the profound nature of relationships, what they simply called human beings.

Among Native Americans it is disgraceful to raise one's head or voice above the group, to separate or distinguish oneself from the unity of the group. While this may hold down individual initiative, it also serves as a force for unity within the tribe.

Dialogue is like the circle. Dialogue is a conversation that seeks unity of thought, unity of understanding and unity of action. These are not achieved by a competition between you and me, but rather through the pursuit of a solution that represents the interests and harmony of "we."

THE HIERARCHY OF PURPOSE: FOUNDATION OF DIALOGUE

Some years ago I attended a workshop on marriage. The presenters used a diagram to illustrate the relationship between husband and wife. At the top of the pyramid they placed God. At the two corners the husband and wife. The point of the triangle was to illustrate that the closer each partner came to God, the closer they came to each other. This simple device always impressed me as representing a profound truth. The closer two people are to a common purpose, a common set of values and beliefs, the closer they come to each other.

What is a comparable unifying force in your work place?

_____

_____

Shared purpose may be something as basic as helping to achieve the survival of your company. It may be a genuine dedication to serving your customers. It may be any mission to which you and your team members are dedicated. The degree to which we lack common purpose is the degree to which we are likely to remain at the bottom of the pyramid, focused on our self, in pursuit of our individual needs. If we are focused only on our personal needs our conversation will tend toward debate, and we will be motivated to win all we can.

As we achieve common purpose, the nature of our motivation and conversation changes. We move from simply trying to win or convince the other person to teaching, sharing, understanding, learning, and serving as we move up the pyramid to a condition of genuine dialogue.

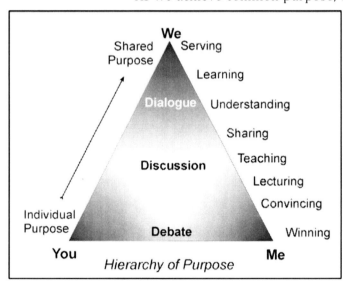

Imagine a congress in which every representative had no self-interest, no concern about his or her election, no concern about winning any personal or party victory. Rather, every member was focused on only one purpose, the collective, shared good of the country. In a true attitude of service, they would seek deep understanding and meaning, striving to make decisions that would be in the best interests of the country. The entire spirit would be transformed, the quality of decision would accelerate, and the country would benefit.

THE COST OF THINKING ALONE

Where in the organization are the most costly quality problems? Are they the defect caused on the factory floor? Are they the missed sales opportunity? Or, are they in conference rooms and offices where managers and executives make decisions? The choice to enter a different type of business, or the decision to select a new chief executive, or the decision to produce one product over another or to buy one type of equipment over another – the quality of these decisions, which will never appear on a Six Sigma project chart or process control graph, are the greatest opportunity for quality and cost improvement.

One of the more amazing realities of recent corporate history is the much discussed collapse of the Enron Corporation. This failure can be described in many ways - a failure of corporate ethics, poor strategic judgment, or outright stealing. But, how did this happen? The Board of Directors of Enron was highly regarded as a model of corporate Board composition. Only two insiders served on the Enron board. No corporation could have had a more financially competent and experienced board. The list included a former Stanford Dean of the Business School who was an accounting professor, the former CEO of an insurance company, the former CEO of an international bank, a hedge fund manager, a prominent Asian financier, and an economist who is the former head of the U.S. government's Commodity Futures Trading Commission. Yet the members of this board have claimed to have been confused by Enron's financial transactions.[19]

How could this group of experienced and respected individuals look over books of a corporation that were so complicated and confused that no analyst could figure out where the money was coming from or where it was going, and thousands of deals were being done that amounted to little more than a shell game of moving money and accounting entries around to give the appearance of profits where there were none?

Jeffrey A. Sonnenfeld writing in the Harvard Business Review[20] said "We need to consider not only how we structure the work of a board but also how we manage the social system a board actually is. We'll be fighting the wrong war if we simply tighten procedural rules for boards and ignore their more pressing need – to be strong, high-functioning work groups whose members trust and challenge one another and engage directly with senior managers on critical issues facing corporations."

Was the Board of Directors engaging in dialogue? Were they thinking deeply and understanding the meaning of the facts presented to

---

[19] "What Makes Great Boards Great", Jeffrey A. Sonnenfeld, Harvard Business Review, September, 2002, p.108.

[20] J. A. Sonnenfeld, Harvard Business Review, September, 2002, p.106.

them? Of course they were not. Rather there was a classic case of "group think" in which even the most analytic board members did not question the facts presented to them, did not dig deep to understand how and why the numbers presented could make sense. Perhaps it was the simple fact that each person around the table had so much respect for the others that they were saying to them "Well, if it makes sense to him, it must make sense." Perhaps this was a case in which a "court jester" was needed, someone to ask the absurd questions, someone who could display complete lack of respect and ask "why "or "how could that be" or request other members of the Board to explain where the money was coming from.

Over and over again in corporate and government history, there are cases of major decisions being made that completely overlook some simple fact and lead to extremely costly decisions. One petroleum company admitted to me that they had invested approximately one billion dollars exploring for oil in a land-locked African country. When they finally found oil, someone asked the obvious question, "How are we going to get it out of the country?" Incredibly, there was no possible way to transport the oil to market. One billion dollars had been wasted because no one had asked an extremely obvious question. These were smart people. How does that happen?

It happens because they are engaged in group-think, acquiescing to someone else and failing to engage in dialogue.

THE BEHAVIORAL CHARACTERISTICS OF DIALOGUE

There are eight key characteristics of groups engaged in a process of dialogue versus those engaged in a process of debate. There is no particular order in which they occur; rather they tend to be parts of a "whole-system" in which the parts reinforce each other.

The following eight characteristics are patterns of behavior of either open or closed human systems or cultures.

1. LISTENING VERSUS CONVINCING:

When you walk into a debate, your mind is set on convincing the judges or audience of the superiority of your point of view. You plan your "arguments," and a great debater voices those arguments in the most convincing manner possible. She speaks with the voice of certainty and authority. The debater has already planned her rebuttal to the expected arguments of the "opponent." This is the way the debate game is played and won. The purpose of a debate is not for the parties to engage in learning. Rather it is to convince the audience that one participant has a superior position and has most skillfully argued that position.

When the motive of conversation is convincing, there is little learning because altering your view would be a sign of weakness, almost an admission that your position is inferior. This would signal defeat.

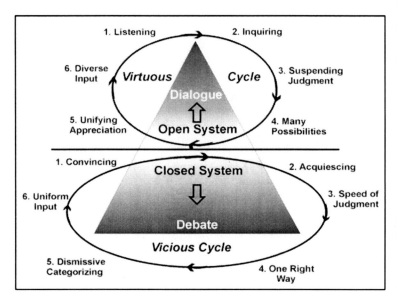

When the motive of a conversation is to listen and to learn, there can be no thought of winning or losing. There is no external audience to convince in a dialogue. You are the audience, the team is the audience, and the purpose is to gain knowledge, understanding, and meaning, and this does not result from authoritatively arguing pre-packaged positions. It derives from listening and thinking together.

We have presidential debates. We don't have presidential dialogues. Which skill will be most relevant and useful to a president confronted with complex issues? Perhaps we should have presidential dialogues to help us select the best candidate.

Everyone has a story, a life history, a life of experiences and knowledge gained, that is different than our own. In dialogue you seek to understand the story of others.

2. INQUIRING VERSUS ACQUIESCING:

Groups in a closed system are likely to be extremely accepting of the views of its members, particularly when those views are expressed by the person in power or expressed framed in the legitimacy of their ideology. This acquiescence avoids the intellectual inquiry, the asking of questions that are the fundamental tool of learning.

Groups who are not engaged in dialogue are highly likely to simply accept a position when legitimized by an accepted ideology, without considering the deep meaning or significance of the position. Good decision-making requires forward thinking, anticipation, considering steps two, three, and four going forward. A culture of debate, in which members of a group acquiesce to power or ideology, blinds the group to the consequences of their decisions.

Inquiry is the foundation of science. Without inquiry, asking questions, there would be no science or human progress. Inquiring minds, questioning minds, seek meaning, significance and underlying truths. The ability to ask questions, to ask the simple question "why?" is the first skill of acquiring wisdom. There is no more important member of a group than the person who recognizes when it is important to ask "why?" It is not at all unusual for groups to be headed off in a direction that no one questions, but neither can anyone explain why they are headed in this direction.

3. SUSPENDING JUDGMENT VERSUS SPEED OF JUDGMENT

A judgment is something that comes "down" at the end of a "trial." If a judge or jury entered a trial with a judgment already in their mind, we would demand that they be disqualified. We ask judges and juries to suspend judgments, to hear all sides, to reflect, and to consider alternative explanations

Healthcare professionals, perhaps more than others, should have a tendency to suspend judgment until they have sufficient data to support an hypothesis. When a patient walks into a hospital or clinic, he or she enters an area where data is quickly being gathered and judgments are being made. Hopefully, the process of dialogue within the clinic or diagnostic area will not be so hasty as to prevent alternative views to be considered and full data to be gathered.

Dialogue is intended to achieve profound understanding, to find new meaning, to explore new and creative solutions, and to create consensus among a group. In order to achieve these things, it is essential that we participate in a period of suspended judgment. We agree to withhold judgment.

In the dominant Western culture we have difficulty suspending judgment. But this is not true of all cultures. A friend of mine worked for a time with native people in the South Pacific Islands. She was a clinical psychologist who specialized in group therapy. She was very skilled at group dynamics, at least from the perspective of her culture. She went to work with a group of local island leaders, the elders of the people in that region. They came together and the topic that required discussion was put forth. There was then a long period of silence in which no one said anything. She felt like it was five minutes, but it was probably more like one minute. In a fast-talking culture like ours, time moves very slowly when there is silence in a group. After a while she put on her "facilitator's hat" and said "Well, why don't we talk about it. We could each share how we feel about this issue." The village elder raised his head and said softly to her "Here we first think about something. Then, once we have thought, we speak."

How often have you found yourself first speaking and then attempting to think about what you wish to say while your lips are already in motion? These native people, as a cultural norm, practiced suspending judgment.

4. ONE "RIGHT WAY" VERSUS OPEN TO ALTERNATIVES

One enters a debate with a position. One enters dialogue with questions. In debate one defends one's position and argues one's position. In dialogue one defends nothing and questions everything in a search for meaning and importance.

In an authoritarian culture there is little consideration of alternatives precisely because the more alternatives are considered, the more questioning must occur. The more questioning that occurs, the more one undermines the assumptions of authoritarian control – the leader knows and you obey. Hence, all democracies, to survive, must be open systems.

A group engaged in open-systems thinking will consider more alternatives because it is precisely from that consideration that learning will occur and creative, or previously impossible, alternatives will emerge. In the process of dialogue there is a joy in discovering new alternatives; like a child discovering a present under the Christmas tree, the group enjoys the thrill of discovery.

The more authoritarian and the more ideological the group, the lower the level of acceptance of diverse points of view will be, and therefore they are more likely to make major misjudgments. A belief in a "right way" can close our eyes to the possibilities of other courses of action. Dialogue implies keeping our minds open, like keeping our eyes and ears open to the sights and sounds in our environment.

5. Unifying Appreciation versus Dismissive Categorizing

Order makes sense out of things. We therefore seek order in conversation. Are we at the beginning or end? Is the conversation hostile or friendly, intelligent or dumb, interesting or boring? There are a hundred ways that we can categorize people, comments, or entire conversations. How we categorize contributions to conversation will have an impact on our ability to enter a meaningful dialogue.

When we hear a comment we do not like, one that differs from our understanding or point of view, we may have a tendency to place that in a category, or place the entire person in a category. This has become unfortunately common in recent years, and points of view are dismissed with "Oh, he is just one of those liberals (or conservatives)."

Imagine that you are in a team meeting and you are discussing how the process of learning and development can be improved. A young woman who has been employed for only a couple of months speaks up and says, "I thought people would be friendlier when I first came to work here. I thought people would help each other more." The manager of this group, somewhat uncomfortable with this expression of personal feelings and emotion thinks to himself, "Well, she just said that because she is young and inexperienced." By placing the young woman and her comment in the category of "young and inexperienced," he alleviates his need to deal with her comment in a meaningful way. He can now move on to listen to comments he may find more comfortable.

How else could the manager think about this remark? He could have thought to appreciate the truth in her comment. For example, he could have said, "I know that it is important when you first come to work that you feel that people want to help you succeed. And, I think you are making the point that we learn well when we help each other, whether we are new or old on the job." By acknowledge the truth or value in the young woman's comment he has created a unifying bond, the opposite of alienation. This appreciative comment will make her more comfortable and more likely to contribute in the future.

6. Uniform Input versus Diverse Input

In a culture of debate, the participants tend to welcome input that reinforces their view and reject or even disparage input that is from a diverse perspective. Each time this happens, the possibility of future diverse input is reduced.

Debate is usually between two people, but it can just as well be between groups. In companies debate can be between the marketing and manufacturing groups or between operating managers and staff managers. More than once I have sat in meetings when some request or suggestion came from that "other" group, the other corner of the triangle, and was rejected immediately, without any genuine consideration, simply because it was one of those "typical" comments by those other people.

A group of corporate decision makers who are all engineers, or all finance managers, or who all come from the same industry or corporate culture, are similarly likely to become a closed system, reinforcing each other's views. One of the advantages of the push for diverse boards and diverse management teams is simply that minorities or women, not conditioned to the same corporate culture and assumptions are more likely to ask the questions that force the group to think about the meaning of what they are doing.

One of the perceptions that will cause members of a group to stay in the corners of the triangle is the perception that those who are unlike us have little to offer. If one is trained as an engineer and the primary work of the organization is engineering, it is normal to value the ideas of other engineers. On senior management teams there will typically be several operating managers who are trained and have risen from the area of core competence of the organization, such as engineering. But there will also be a finance manager, a human resource manager, possibly an attorney or others. The nature of conversation is often prejudiced by the value placed on these areas of expertise, independent of the actual merit of a contribution by a team member.

The assumption of dialogue is that the group is seeking the best understanding, the best solution, for the combined interests of the group. This can only happen if the members of the group can learn to look beyond their own filters that differentiate the contributions of one individual over another.

CHAPTER 20

IMPROVING TEAM DYNAMICS

The purpose of this chapter is to improve relationships within the team that will allow open, honest, and trusting communications among team members.

OBJECTIVES

1. To assess the dynamics of communication among team members.

2. To build trust among team members.

3. To get to know team members as individuals with unique preferences, fears and desires.

TEAM DYNAMICS ASSESSMENT

Complete the following team dynamics assessment and have your coach compile the results and feed them back to the team.

TRUST:

1. I trust that when I offer my opinion to the group I will be heard and respected.

1_____2_____3_____4_____5
Not at all   Somewhat   Very Much

2. I trust that other members of the group are offering their honest opinions to the group.

1_____2_____3_____4_____5
Not at all   Somewhat   Very Much

3. I will not be "put-down" for offering an opinion that may be very different from others in the group.

1_____2_____3_____4_____5
Not at all   Somewhat   Very Much

4. Our discussion and opinions will stay inside this team and not be shared outside the team or used against another member.

1_____2_____3_____4_____5
Not at all   Somewhat   Very Much

HONEST STRAIGHT TALK:

5. Members of my team say what they mean and mean what they say.

1_____2_____3_____4_____5
Not at all   Somewhat   Very Much

6. Members of the group are truthful, not only when discussing facts, but also when discussing what they personally think and feel.

1_____2_____3_____4_____5
Not at all   Somewhat   Very Much

7. Team members are not only honest in what they say, but are also honest in what they don't say. In other words, if they have information or an opinion, I can trust that they will share it openly and honestly.

1_____2_____3_____4_____5

Not at all   Somewhat   Very Much

8. I feel comfortable being completely open and honest with my team in expressing my concerns, ideas, opinions and feelings.

1_____2_____3_____4_____5
Not at all   Somewhat   Very Much

EMPATHY:

9. The last time I shared a personal concern or problem with my team I feel that they understood my feelings.

1_____2_____3_____4_____5
Not at all   Somewhat   Very Much

10. Members of this team genuinely care about the well-being of other members of the team.

1_____2_____3_____4_____5
Not at all   Somewhat   Very Much

11. If a member of the team shares a need for help, other members of the team will volunteer to provide that help.

1_____2_____3_____4_____5
Not at all   Somewhat   Very Much

12. Team members look out for each other, not just themselves.

1_____2_____3_____4_____5
Not at all   Somewhat   Very Much

UNITY OF PURPOSE:

13. Members of my team share a common purpose and define "winning" in the same way.

1_____2_____3_____4_____5
Not at all   Somewhat   Very Much

14. When we meet we are working on the same agenda, and team members do not have hidden or personal agendas that interfere with the purpose of the group.

1_____2_____3_____4_____5
Not at all   Somewhat   Very Much

15. There is a high "sense of purpose" on the team, a desire to accomplish our mission.

1_____2_____3_____4_____5
Not at all   Somewhat   Very Much

16. Our team feels united, as if we are working together as one cohesive unit.

1_____2_____3_____4_____5
Not at all   Somewhat   Very Much

APPRECIATION OF DIVERSITY:

17. In some ways I am different from other members of my team. Other team members recognize and appreciate these differences.

1_____2_____3_____4_____5
Not at all   Somewhat   Very Much

18. Members of the team speak in different "voices", some more assertive, some more quiet or reserved. All members are heard equally for the content of what they have to say, rather than how loudly they speak.

1_____2_____3_____4_____5
Not at all   Somewhat   Very Much

19. In every group there is a dominant culture. There are usually individuals who represent a sub-culture or minority culture. Our team listens and respects the views of those representing these different cultures with respect and understanding.

1_____2_____3_____4_____5
Not at all   Somewhat   Very Much

20. Diversity of experience, perspectives and opinions is an asset to a team. It is the expression of this diversity that prevents "group-think." My team is diverse, and diverse views are expressed and well received by the team.

1_____2_____3_____4_____5
Not at all   Somewhat   Very Much

HOW DID YOUR TEAM SCORE?

Compile the average scores for each item and for each category. There is a potential score of twenty for each category.

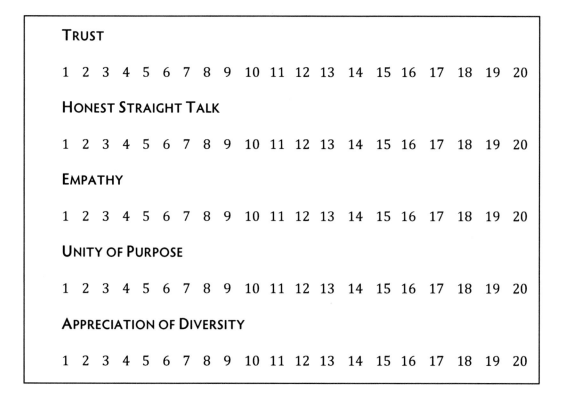

TRUST

1 2 3 4 5 6 7 8 9 10 11 12 13 14 15 16 17 18 19 20

HONEST STRAIGHT TALK

1 2 3 4 5 6 7 8 9 10 11 12 13 14 15 16 17 18 19 20

EMPATHY

1 2 3 4 5 6 7 8 9 10 11 12 13 14 15 16 17 18 19 20

UNITY OF PURPOSE

1 2 3 4 5 6 7 8 9 10 11 12 13 14 15 16 17 18 19 20

APPRECIATION OF DIVERSITY

1 2 3 4 5 6 7 8 9 10 11 12 13 14 15 16 17 18 19 20

DEBRIEF:

In your team meeting, discuss the following questions and reach consensus on ways you can improve the inter-personal dynamics of your team. It is very important to keep in mind that every team, every family, every community, every group of human beings, can improve how they deal with each other. The purpose is not to conclude that you are either good or bad. The purpose is to make continuous improvement in the human dynamics of your team.

When debriefing, agree on the rule "No one is to blame, or we are all to blame!"

1. Which category produced the highest score?
   a. Why do you believe you scored well in this category?

b. What specific behavior contributed to this score?

_____

_____

_____

_____

1. Which category produced the lowest score?
    a. Why do you believe you scored low in this category?
    b. What specific behavior contributed to this low score?

_____

_____

_____

_____

2. Review the individual items and the scores for each item in the other categories.
    a. These scores suggest that we could improve what behavior to improve the inter-personal dynamics within our team?

_____

_____

_____

_____

IMPROVING THE INTER-PERSONAL DYNAMICS OF YOUR TEAM

Perhaps the first and most important thing any team can do to improve the dynamics within the team is to periodically "process" their own functioning as a team. Stop and think, reflect, and then discuss how your team is functioning. Doing this periodically, in an open and honest way is the most essential step in improving the inter-personal dynamics of any team.

Over the past years many exercises have been developed to improve the dynamics of teams. Some are done within the normal team setting, and others are experiential exercises that require going off-site for outdoor, more physical experiences.

One of the most effective exercises I have experienced was when a company leadership team decided to take on a service project as a team. This company was in a construction related business. They knew how to build things. They found that the local YWCA/YMCA needed to reconstruct the building that had been donated to them. Over a six month period this management team worked together to reconstruct the building. After doing this, the team reported that they learned more about each other, came to trust each other, and had better feelings toward each other than ever before. This was a true "action-learning" experience that both improved the performance and "spirit" of the team, and also improved the company's relations in the community.

TRUST BUILDING EXERCISES

3. TWO TRUTHS AND A LIE

This is an easy and effective first exercise. It is an "ice-breaker" and a simple get-to-know each other game. The purpose of the game is to learn something about each team member that you would not learn through the routine of team meetings focused on work.

Directions: Ask each member of the team to write down three things. Two of them are true things that other members of the group are not likely to know. The third one is a lie.

Then go around the room and have each person read their three things. Ask everyone to guess which one is the lie. After everyone guesses, then ask the person to share which are true and which was a lie.

Debrief: Make it simple. Ask the group what was the most surprising thing they learned about a team member.

4. IF I MADE A MOVIE...

This exercise is somewhat similar to the above, but it gets to a more serious level of knowing other members of the group. To share hopes, dreams and fears requires trust in other members. This is another practice session in building trust.

Facilitator: It is important that group members share their stories voluntarily. Some may not be comfortable sharing and they should be invited, but not pressured to share.

Directions: If I made a movie and it was about my life, what scene would be a defining moment in the movie? It can be tragic or heroic. Describe the scene and why it would be a defining moment of my life. This can be an actual scene or one that you make up to illustrate a key event or transition in your life. If you were casting an actor to play you in this movie, who would you cast in your role?

Ask each member of the group to spend ten to fifteen minutes defining the scene and which actor would play them in the movie.

Then, ask members to volunteer to share their scene and the actor. Ask them what this scene tells us that is important about their life.

Debrief: After each person has shared their story, ask the group "What have we learned about another team member that helps us understand them better?"

Straight Talk Exercises

Trust and honesty are two sides of the same coin. The more honest we are, the more we will be trusted by others. The kind of honesty that we are concerned with on the team is not honesty about telling lies. It is more about "straight-talk," the honesty that is sharing what you really feel, saying what is on your mind. Group cohesion and group decision-making are often hindered by members of the group simply not "honestly" sharing what they think and feel. This type of honesty may also be called "being open" or willing to share what is inside of you.

5. The Truths I Deny Myself

One of the ways that we are not entirely honest is not being honest with ourselves. We all (at least most of us) tell ourselves little falsehoods to avoid confronting something we may want to avoid confronting. The purpose of this exercise is to initiate openness and sharing among team members.

Directions: Ask each team member to write down two different ways that "I fool myself" or "I am not completely honest with myself." It is important that the facilitator model, give examples, him or herself. So start by sharing two things you, the facilitator, do to fool yourself. For example:

I tell myself I am trying to lose weight and then I sneak ice cream with pure maple syrup on top, late at night before I go to bed.

I am trying to save money by spending less, yet I cannot resist buying some latest gadget because it is the newest, best whatever, even though I know I don't really need it.

Give the group five or ten minutes to write down their little falsehoods that they tell themselves. Then ask the members of the group to share. It is best not to go around the room, but just ask for volunteers so members who are uncomfortable don't feel pressured.

When others are sharing, no one else should make any disapproving comment ("Oh my God! I can't believe you do that!") Remember that the purpose of this exercise is to confront the common habit of denial within all of us.

Debrief: The facilitator should point out that we all have things in common. What are the common habits that we shared?

Ask the group, what does this tendency to not confront things, even to ourselves, tell us about how we communicate or work together?

Do we fail to be open and honest with others for the same reasons we may fail to be honest with ourselves?

UNITY OF PURPOSE

Teams are most successful when the members of the team share common goals and common purpose. Your team developed a charter that included a purpose statement, and this should be your shared purpose. But we all have our own purpose, our own goals or concerns, and sometimes these personal issues are more dominant than our collective purpose.

6. THE PURPOSE DIAGRAM

This exercise is intended to elicit personal reflection on the part of team members and develop understanding of the goals we have in common.

Directions: This exercise has three parts: first, private reflection; second, developing an "affinity diagram"; third, debrief. This exercise can be used as practice in developing an affinity diagram, a skill that will be useful in other activities.

Explain to the group that we will use an "affinity diagram" to share our understanding of our own purpose and goals and how they are common or different.

Explain what an affinity diagram is: *A brainstorming and decision technique designed to generate and then sort a large number of ideas into related groups in a visual display.* Ask the group to follow the following steps to generate this diagram.

Step 1: Describe the Problem or Issue: The issue in this case is "why are we here?" What is our goal or purpose that brings us together as a team? What do I hope to gain, achieve or experience by participating on this team?

Step 2: Generate ideas: Distribute small pads of post-it-notes to each member of the team. Ask them to write down, each on a separate note, as many ideas that answer the question as they can think of. The ideas can be big ones or small ones. Give the group ten minutes to think about and write down their ideas.

Step 3: Display the ideas. Post the ideas on a wall, or a table in a *random* manner. Just get them up so they can all be seen. Then ask them to start studying all of the ideas that have been posted. IMPORTANT: ask them to do this and the next step in SILENCE. This is hard for most teams. Explain that this may be a new experience, but we will learn that sometimes the team can learn and decide without talking at all.

Step 4: Sort the ideas into related groups. Ask the team members physically sort the cards into groupings, **without talking**, using the following process:

- Start by looking for two ideas that seem related in some way. Place them together in a column off to one side.
- Look for ideas that are related to those you've already set aside and add them to that group.
- Look for other ideas that are related to each other and establish new groups. This process is repeated until the team has placed all of the ideas in groups.

NOTE: Ideally, all of the ideas can be sorted into related groups. If there are some "loners" that don't fit any of the groups, don't force them into groupings where they don't belong. Let them stand alone under their own headers or under a "miscellaneous" heading.

Step 5: Create header cards for the groups. A header is an idea that captures the essential link among the ideas contained in a group of cards. This idea is written on a single card or post-it-note and must consist of a phrase or sentence that clearly conveys the meaning, even to people who are not on the team. The team develops headers for the groups by...

- Finding already existing cards within the groups that will serve well as headers and placing them at the top of the group of related cards.
- Alternatively, discussing and agreeing on the wording of cards created specifically to be headers.
- Once you have completed the affinity diagram ask the group to discuss what they learned from doing this. Ask the following questions:

What does this tell us about the goals and purpose that we share?

What does this tell us about how we are different in our goals and purpose?

Does this tell us anything about how we function as a team, or how we should function as a team?

Summarize by pointing out the importance of common purpose and how this is present or how it needs to be developed by the team.

APPRECIATION OF DIVERSITY:

The subject of diversity in the workplace is one that has been addressed by many forms of training. Most of this has focused on two issues: race and gender. Over the past fifty years our workplace has changed dramatically in the increased number of women and African-Americans, Hispanics and Asians in the workplace. There are many specialized workshops to address how we respond to these changes.

You may think of the following exercise as merely an introduction to this subject, and an opportunity to recognize, understand and appreciate all of the different forms of diversity that are present on our team.

7. WE ARE ALL DIFFERENT – WE ARE ALL THE SAME

Among the members of any team there are similarities and differences that affect the way we view problems and solutions. These differences also affect our manner of speech, our emotions, and how we interpret events. The purpose of this exercise is to share some of those differences among team members and how they influence our behavior.

Directions: Explain that the purpose of this exercise is to recognize some of the differences -- the unique qualities and experience -- of each member of our team.

- Ask the team members to spend ten to fifteen minutes alone, reflecting on how they may be different from all or the majority of other team members. These differences may be ethnic, age, gender, religion, work experience, education, personality or other life experience. Ask them to write down three ways that they are unique or different.
- The facilitator will then ask that each member share his or her three differences.
- The facilitator will instruct all the team members to listen well and think about how the differences being described present the team with an asset, some value or virtue that can be appreciated and contribute to the team.
- Immediately after an individual shares his or her differences, the facilitator will ask the group "How do you feel those qualities or experiences can be an asset to our team?" Let the group share their thoughts for a few moments and then go on to the next person.

Debrief: After everyone has shared and received this appreciation from the group, ask the team to spend three minutes just thinking about and reflecting on what they heard. Then ask the group the following questions:

- How did the group's response to your diversity cause you to feel?
- How did it make you feel about the team in general?
- How may what you learned affect the future behavior of the team?

Team Commitment

The purpose of this exercise is to help the team explore the meaning of "commitment" to the team and each other and to practice giving and receiving feedback on their commitment.

There are four stages of this exercise: first, brainstorming indicators of commitment; second, private assessment of each individual's demonstration of those indicators; third, sharing and processing that feedback; and fourth, reflection and sharing commitments to future behavior. The exercise is structured to provide confidential feedback and minimize the possibility of painful confrontations that sometimes occur over this issue.

You will need a large number of post-it-notes, preferably of the same color so as not to indicate which member is providing which feedback.

Directions:

1. **Identifying Indicators:** Brainstorm what "commitment" means in a team setting. Ask the group, "How do you know it when you see it?" Or, "What pinpointed behaviors demonstrate that a member is committed to the success of the team?" Also, ask "What behavior indicates personal commitment to each other?"

- Generate a list of as many ideas as come to mind within ten minutes. This will probably be ten to twenty indicators such as "attends meetings regularly;" "participates in problem-solving and discussion;" or, "follows through on action items."
- Combine similar indicators. Your goal is to get down to only five indicators. Be sure that they are still pinpointed, observable behavior.
- Vote on the five that are most important and most reliable indicators of commitment to the team.

2. **Assessing Fellow Team Members:** On the following page is a sheet to record each person's evaluation of the other members of the team.

- Place the five indicators across the five columns titled "Indicators of Commitment." Each member should have a sheet like that on the following page. This sheet should be kept private by that member.
- Place the names of the other team members down the left hand column.

- Ask each member to rate each other member on each of these qualities using a ten point scale. You can give the team fifteen minutes to do this in the meeting, or (and this is preferable) give them time between meetings to think about their assessment and complete the ratings during the time between this and the next meeting.

3. **Sharing Feedback:** The purpose of the following is to allow for each team member to receive absolutely frank and honest feedback without public discussion that could be painful or humiliating. The facilitator should keep in mind that it is often difficult for members to give public feedback and this leads to individuals receiving little or no feedback on their behavior.

- On a wall, the facilitator should make a table, somewhat like that on the following page, with the team member's names to the left in a column, and column headings for each of the indicators.
- Pass out post-it-notes to the team members. Ask them to write their ratings on the adhesive side of the post-it-note. It will help if they write the indicator on the visible side, such as "Attendance." This way, when they are placed on the wall, the side with the indicator will be visible and the rating will not be visible.
- For each other team member, each participant will write their rating on five notes, one for each indicator. They will then place them on the wall in the appropriate column and row.
- When all the notes have been placed on the wall, ask each individual to gather up their notes, keeping track of which indicator they represent. Returning to their seat, they should then average their scores for each item.

4. **Reflection and Commitment:** Give the team fifteen or twenty minutes to read and average their scores. Ask them to consider sharing the following based on the feedback they have received:

- What is one thing you will do in the future to strengthen your commitment to the success of the team?
- What help would you like to receive from other team members in the future?

TEAM COMMITMENT ASSESSMENT

TEAM MEMBER	INDICATORS OF COMMITMENT				

Score each team member on each indicator on a 1 to 10 scale. 1 would indicate that the team member never demonstrates this behavior; 5 that they demonstrate this sometimes; and 10 that they demonstrate this to a very high degree.

GLOSSARY

- **5S:** 5S is a common tool and component of a lean workplace. The Five S program focuses on having visual order, organization, cleanliness and standardization. The results you can expect from a Five S program are: improved profitability, efficiency, service and safety. The 5S's are Sort, Set in order, Shine, Standardize, and Sustain

- **5 Why's:** The 5 Why's is a simple problem-solving technique that helps you to get to the root of a problem quickly. Made popular in the 1970s by the Toyota Production System, the 5 Whys strategy involves looking at any problem and asking: "Why?" and "What caused this problem?"

- **7 Forms of Waste:** Waste is the use of any material or resource beyond what the customer requires and is willing to pay for. Shigeo Shingo identified "Seven" forms of waste (Plus one – The eighth waste, under-utilization of people) These 7 forms of waste are 1) Over production, 2) Inventory, 3) Motion, 4) Waiting, 5) Transportation, 6) Over-processing, 7) Scrap or rework.

- **A3:** An A3 is literally a size of paper (297 × 420 mm). However, it has become popular in lean management as a simple and structured form of problem-solving that can fit on or be displayed on one A3 sized paper.

- **A4:** An A4 is again a size of paper. However, it has become known for an even simpler problem-solving process than an A3. It is a one sheet PDCA cycle problem-solving tool. (see PDCA)

- **ABC Model:** This is a model for changing behavior, whether at work or in any setting. It stands for Antecedents, Behavior and Consequences. Doing an ABC analysis is a way of analyzing why someone may be behaving in a given way and what can be done to change that behavior.

- **Action Planning:** After deciding on a solution to a problem, a team should develop an action plan that clearly states what steps are going to be taken to implement a solution; who is going to do them; and, when are they going to be done by. Action plans are generally reviewed at each team meeting.

- **Affinity Diagram:** An affinity diagram is a component of brainstorming in which participants write ideas down on Post-it-Notes, then put them on a wall, and then silently organize them into like blocks of notes.

- **Antecedents:** A stimulus that precedes a behavior and acts as a stimulus or cue for that behavior to occur.

- **Balanced Scorecard:** A team or management scorecard that includes four types of measures: Financial, learning and development, customer satisfaction and process measures. This concept was developed and promoted in a book by Kaplan and Norton.

- **Behavior Analysis:** The application of behavioral psychology to behavior in a natural setting. Also referred to as *behavior management* or *performance management.*
- **Behavior Management:** A term used to describe the application of behavior analysis or behavior modification in the work place. It generally involves seeking to employ positive reinforcement to increase the strength and learning of desired behavior.
- **Behavioral psychology:** That school of psychology developed by B.F. Skinner and others that states that behavior is learned a function of the contingencies of reinforcement in the environment. Behavioral psychology is based on scientific or the experimental analysis of behavior in which antecedent stimuli and consequences to behavior are controlled and modified and the resulting changes in rate of behavior are monitored.
- **Brainstorming:** Brainstorming is one component of both problem-solving and group decision-making. It is a way to bring out the creativity of the group by focusing on generating ideas while not judging them. There are many methods of brainstorming but they all include the element of suspending judgment, allowing, even encouraging, wild and crazy ideas so that each idea may stimulate another.
- **Cause and Effect:** A cause and effect diagram is also known as a fishbone diagram because it looks something like the skeleton of a fish. At the backbone of the diagram is the definition of a problem. Then each of the major parts of the skeleton are labeled (and this is only one way of many) People, Process, Materials, Equipment, Information. Then you use this to brainstorm possible causes under each of these categories.
- **CEDAC:** Cause and Effect Diagrams with the Addition of Cards. This is simply a very large cause and effect diagram placed on a wall in a prominent place, such as a hallway where employees pass by, and there are two color cards, one for problems and the other for solutions. Employees are encouraged to add problem or solution cards as they think of them. This creates an on-going brainstorming process.
- **Command Decisions:** Command decisions are those made by one individual. This is generally considered most efficient when time is a priority and/or the one individual has superior expertise. Command decision is considered the traditional military model of decision-making and battlefield conditions are the environment where this is most appropriate.
- **Consensus Decisions:** Consensus decisions are those decisions that are owned by an entire group and the entire group agrees on a decision after giving everyone an opportunity to speak and be heard respectfully. Consensus decision-making assumes that the formal leader is willing to delegate the decision authority to the group. Consensus decisions are more time consuming but result in greater commitment from the group.
- **Consultative Decisions:** Consultative decisions are those in which one individual owns and controls the decision, but does not make it alone. Rather the individual

consults with those who have knowledge, who care, or who must act to implement the decision.

- **Continuous Improvement:** Continuous improvement is one of the fundamental ideas of lean management. It is based on the simple idea that every process can always be improved in some increment. It is a process in which all employees engaged in the work are encouraged to participate in thinking about better ways to do things, conducting experiments, and agreeing on improved standard work.
- **Cycle Time:** A cycle time is the time from the beginning to the end of a work process. There are generally two types of cycle time: CT = The actual Cycle Time from beginning to end, and VCT=Value Adding Cycle Time. In other words, if you look at your daily work process, that may be eight hours, how much of that time is actually adding value to your customers? It is usually a fraction of the actual time. In lean terms, the remaining time is considered "waste."
- **Debate:** Debate is a form of conversation in which two or more parties have predetermined positions on a matter and are attempting to convince others that they are correct and the others are wrong. The participants are not willing to learn from each other or change their positions.
- **Dialogue:** Dialogue is the art of thinking together rather than thinking alone. It is often considered the opposite of debate, a conversation in which all parties are seeking to learn, to discover truth together.
- **DIMPABAC:** This is an acronym representing one problem-solving model. *Define* the problem to be solved; *Inquire* with all those who have facts regarding the problem to gain different understanding and insight; *Measure* actual performance on the problem; *Principles* should be defined that are important to understanding this problem and its solution; *Analyze* the data and causes of the problem; *Brainstorm* solutions to the problem; Agree to *Act* on a solution; *Control* and standardize the process and evaluate results.
- **Empathy:** Empathy is the capacity to recognize and, to some extent, share feelings (such as sadness or happiness) that are being experienced by another. Empathy is one of the effective listening skills that enables another person to express their thoughts and feelings.
- **Facilitation:** Facilitation is the skill or art of helping others participate in group problem-solving or decision-making. There are a set of skills that are components of effective facilitation and these include clarifying topics, active listening, conflict resolution, and helping a group reach and clarify a decision.
- **Feedback:** Feedback is information on performance that is "fed back" to the group or individual in control of that performance. Feedback is not necessarily positive or negative, but may simply be information on performance. Feedback is the most essential element of all systems of human performance.
- **Fishbone Diagrams:** See cause and effect diagrams.
- **Four to One:** The practice of recognizing four desirable behaviors to every one negative. Based on the research of Dr. Ogden Lindsley who found that the optimum rate of positive to negative in classrooms was 3.57 to 1.

- **Gemba:** Gemba is a Japanese word meaning "the real place where work gets done." It refers to the place where value is created in a work system. Being "on-the-spot" is another term meaning being where the work gets done. This is an important concept in lean management and it expresses the value of managers "going and seeing" what is really happening where the work is being done.
- **Gemba Walk:** The Gemba walk is simply that act of managers talking a walk around the work place and observing, learning, from those doing the work. In manufacturing it is recommended that plant managers take frequent Gemba walks to be in touch with the real work.
- **Kaizen:** Kaizen is the Japanese word for continuous improvement. It is one of the core philosophies and practices of lean management. Kaizen is intended to be practiced by all employees, at every level, engaged in every work process in the organization.
- **Kaizen Event:** A kaizen event is an intensified and short effort to make a major improvement in a process. It generally involves a cross-functional team of employees who work for a period, such as a week, studying a process to solve a problem and make a recommendation at the end of that period.
- **Leader Standard Work:** Leader standard work (LSW) is a process by which standard work, activities that are to be done daily, weekly or monthly, are defined by or for a manager. LSW involves the regular review of the completion and lessons learned from these activities by the manager at the next level above.
- **Lean Management:** Lean management is the set of management and work practices derived from the Toyota Production System (TPS). These include the elimination of waste, continuous improvement, and involvement of all employees in improvement activities. Lean and TPS are not a static set of practices, but are continually evolving as lessons are learned from application in different settings such as health care.
- **Lean Process:** A lean process is one in which every step adds value, speed through the process is optimized, there are no interruptions or re-work, and those who work in the process seek continuous improvement.
- **Continuous Improvement:** Continuous improvement is the merger of the lessons from lean management and those learned from the implementation of self-directed teams and the socio-technical system (STS) design of high performance work systems.
- **PDCA Cycle:** The PDCA (Plan, Do, Check and Act) cycle of problem-solving is also known as the Schewhart Cycle after Walter Schewhart a pioneer in the quality field. During the quality movement it was adopted as a common problem-solving model at many companies. The PDCA cycle is best used for relatively simple problems, although you can place many different methods or steps within these four major steps.
- **PDSA:** This is essentially the same as the PDCA cycle of problem-solving: Plan, Do, Study, Act. This is the term used at ThedaCare.
- **Performance Analysis:** A model of problem-solving human behavior. It is based on the work of Robert Mager and Peter Pipe who suggested that we ask "Is the

problem *a can't* do, or a *won't do* problem." In other words, does the individual have the required skill or knowledge, or is it a motivation problem.

- **Performance Management:** This term has two different usages. One is another term to describe behavior management or applied behavior analysis in the work setting. A second describes the process of individual performance appraisal and the development of periodic personal improvement plans, generally negotiated between an employee and his or her manager.
- **Positive Reinforcement:** In behavioral psychology or applied behavior analysis positive reinforcement is the presentation of a stimulus following a behavior that results in a subsequent increase in the rate of that behavior.
- **Process:** A process is a set of related activities that together produce a desired outcome. All processes have both input and output. The process transforms input to a value adding output. Teams are generally organized around, and take responsibility for, a defined process.
- **Process Management Teams:** A team that owns and takes responsibility for the continuous improvement of a defined process.
- **Process Maps:** A visual display of a process that illustrates each step in a process and their chronological relationship to one another. It describes the flow of the process. Process mapping allows a team to define cycle times, identify waste and variances in the process.
- **Process Measures:** Measures of process performance. These measures may be derived from within the process or at the end of a process. For example, if you are cooking a turkey dinner (a process) you may take a measure of the temperature of the meat while it is cooking (a measure within the process), and you may measure the satisfaction of the guests when they are finished eating the turkey (end of process measure).
- **Reflective Listening:** Also known as rephrasing or active listening. Reflective listening is somewhat like holding up a mirror, a reflection, of what you think another person meant to say. For example, "In other words I hear you saying that you enjoy doing that job." This gives the other person the opportunity to say "Well, no, that isn't really what I meant." Or, "Yes, that's right." The other person may clarify and will feel that he or she has genuinely been heard.
- **Scorecards**: A score card is an agreed upon set of metrics that reflect the performance of a team. See "balanced scorecard." Scorecards are best visually displayed and reviewed regularly.
- **Self-Directed Teams:** Also known as autonomous or semi-autonomous teams, self-directed teams take responsibility for managing a process and continuously improving that process. While no team is ultimately "self-managed", the process of self-directed teams seeks to maximize the responsibility and maturity of a team to manage performance. Continuous Improvement is a self-directed team process.
- **Shaping Behavior:** Shaping is a concept of behavior analysis. Shaping is the successive reinforcement of approximations to a terminal goal set of responses or skill. In other words, when your child is first learning to play the piano, you praise

(reinforce) small improvements and effort, rather than waiting for the ultimate performance.

- **SIPOC:** An acronym that stands for Supplier, Input, Process, Output and Customer. This describes the process flow through a team or organization and is a fundamental tool of lean and process improvement.
- **Six Sigma:** An improvement process first developed at Motorola and an extension of the total quality movement. It relies heavily on statistical methods and has been used predominantly in manufacturing. A six sigma process is one in which 99.99966% of the products manufactured are statistically expected to be free of defects (3.4 defects per million).
- **SMED:** Single Minute Exchange of Dies. This is a component of lean manufacturing and was one of the early efforts to eliminate waste from the a core work process in automotive or other metal manufacturing.
- **Socio-Technical Systems (STS):** A process developed, originally at the Tavistock Institute in Great Britain by Fred Emery and Eric Trist to improve both the productivity of the work system while at the same time improving the social system. The theory of STS is that there is one whole-system, comprised of both social and technical components that are interdependent. Failing to change one element sub-optimizes any change effort.
- **Special Cause:** Dr. W. Edwards Deming described the statistical evidence of a process *in control* in which all of the causes of variation are within three standard deviations of the mean. The cause of variation is common to the system and can only be improved by changing the system itself.
- **Standard Work:** A set of activities that have been agreed to be the best way to perform any work activity. Standard work is the best way we know now to perform a work process. However, continuous improvement will find better ways that will then become standard work.
- **Statistical Variation:** A set of statistical recording of performance that define a mean of that set and the variations around that mean.
- **Subject Matter Experts**: (SME's) May be permanent or temporary members of a team who are assigned or recognized to possess expertise in some function or knowledge area that contributes to the performance of the team.
- **Team Charter:** A document that defines a team's purpose, its processes, its customers and the principles by which it will function.
- **TQM:** Total Quality Management, a set of practices that involves a focus on the requirements of customers (or customers), the use of statistical measures of quality performance, teams improving quality and customer service at every level of the organization.
- **Value Stream Mapping:** Mapping the work flow, or processes, in a manner that identifies the points where value is added and non-value adding activities, or waste.
- **Variances or Variation:** A variance may be described statistically, or it may simply be something that deviates or varies from how things should be done in order to meet customer requirements. A variance is a problem.

- **Waste:** Any activity that does not directly add value to the product or service delivered to a customer.
- **Whole-System Architecture:** Another term used for socio-technical systems design in which all elements of an organization's systems are examined together to assess how they enhance or reduce the quality of product or service to customers or customers.

INDEX

ABOUT THE AUTHOR

For the past thirty-five years Lawrence M. Miller has worked to improve the performance of organizations and the skills of their leaders. His expertise is derived from hands on experience creating change in the culture of hundreds of organizations.

He began his work in North Carolina prisons after recognizing that the system in the organization had exactly the opposite of its intended effect – increasing, rather than decreasing, dysfunctional behavior. For four years he worked to redesign the prison system by establishing the first free-economy behind prison walls, where each inmate had to pay rent, maintain a checking account, and pay for everything he desired. This was one of the first applications of *behavior analysis* in the correctional setting.

He has been consulting, writing and speaking about business organization and culture since 1973. He and his firm were one of the early proponents of team-based management and worked with many customers from the senior executive team to include every level and every employee in the organization. Mr. Miller personally coaches the senior management team of many of his customers.

Among his consulting customers have been Allina Health Systems, VON Canada, 3M, Corning, Shell Oil Company, Amoco and Texaco, Shell Chemicals, Air Canada, Eastman Chemicals, Xerox, Harris Corporation, McDonald's and Chick-fil-A, Merck and Upjohn Pharmaceuticals, United Technologies, American Express, and Metropolitan Life.

His website is www.LMMiller.com and his blog is www.ManagementMeditations.com. His email is LMMiller@lmmiller.com.

PREVIOUS PUBLICATIONS

- *Behavior Management: The New Science of Managing People at Work,* John Wiley & Sons, Inc., 1978.
- *American Spirit: Visions of a New Corporate Culture;* William Morrow & Company, Inc., 1984.
- *Barbarians to Bureaucrats: Corporate Life Cycle Strategies;* Clarkson Potter (Crown Books), 1989.
- *From Management to Leadership;* Productivity Press, 1995.
- *Team Management: Creating Systems and Skills for a Team Based Organization;* Miller Howard Consulting Group, (with Jennifer Howard), 1994.
- *Change Management: Creating the Dynamic Organization through Whole System Architecture,* Miller Howard Consulting Group, 1997.
- *Spiritual Enterprise: Building Your Business in the Spirit of Service;* George Ronald Publishers, 2007.
- *Lean Culture – The Leader's Guide;* L. M. Miller Consulting, 2011

SERVICES

SURVEYS

Lean Culture Survey: Survey your employees to determine your degree of conformance to the ten cultural principles of lean culture. This survey can be the basis for planning improvement and engaging employees.

Lean Leadership Survey: Do your leaders support lean culture through their own behavior, modeling the behavior that supports lean culture? This confidential survey is intended to provide private and personal feedback to leaders and serves as a foundation for leadership coaching.

CONSULTING

Mr. Miller works with his clients on long term culture change and lean implementation. He assists with both more revolutionary change, Whole-System Architecture, and with continuous improvement. He works with internal coaches or change agents to prepare and assist them as they coach teams throughout the organization. He also directly coaches the senior leadership teams of his customers.

EXECUTIVE COACHING

Senior managers often can benefit most from one-on-one private coaching and feedback. Mr. Miller has coached senior executives at major corporations such as Honeywell, American Express, Shell and others. This coaching is most often a component of a larger effort to improve the culture of the organization.

TRAINING AND TRAINING MATERIALS

Mr. Miller provides training to internal coaches and senior managers in the process of *Continuous Improvement* and Lean Culture. His Continuous Improvement workbook is accompanied by a complete set of PowerPoint presentation and teaching notes.

SPEAKING ENGAGEMENTS

Mr. Miller has been a popular speaker at hundreds of company and association conferences. He speaks both on lean culture and corporate life-cycles and leadership based on his Barbarians to Bureaucrats book. He also leads leadership workshops to initiate lean culture change.

CPSIA information can be obtained at www.ICGtesting.com
Printed in the USA
LVOW09s2216190214

374461LV00001B/16/P